D1540368

Especially for

From

Date

Bible
Memory
Plan

for

MORNING &
EVENING

BARBOUR BOOKS
An Imprint of Barbour Publishing, Inc.

© 2017 by Barbour Publishing, Inc.

Written and compiled by Jean Fischer.

Print ISBN 978–1–68322–080–0

All rights reserved. No part of this publication may be reproduced or transmitted for commercial purposes, except for brief quotations in printed reviews, without written permission of the publisher.

Daily readings are by Jean Fischer or are adapted from *Spa–"aah" Moments for Women, Today, God Wants You to Know, 3–Minute Devotions for Women, Be Encouraged, God's Heart for You, Discovering God in Everyday Moments.* © by Barbour Publishing, Inc.

Scripture quotations marked NASB are taken from the New American Standard Bible, © 1960, 1962, 1963, 1968, 1971, 1972, 1973, 1975, 1977, 1995 by The Lockman Foundation. Used by permission.

Scripture quotations marked KJV are taken from the King James Version of the Bible.

Scripture quotations marked NKJV are taken from the New King James Version®. Copyright © 1982 by Thomas Nelson. Used by permission. All rights reserved.

Scripture quotations marked NIV are taken from the HOLY BIBLE, NEW INTERNATIONAL VERSION®. NIV®. Copyright © 1973, 1978, 1984, 2011 by Biblica, Inc.™ Used by permission. All rights reserved worldwide.

Scripture quotations marked MSG are from THE MESSAGE. Copyright © by Eugene H. Peterson 1993, 1994, 1995, 1996, 2000, 2001, 2002. Used by permission of NavPress Publishing Group.

Scripture quotations marked ESV are from The Holy Bible, English Standard Version®, copyright © 2001 by Crossway Bibles, a publishing ministry of Good News Publishers. Used by permission. All rights reserved.

Scripture quotations marked NLT are taken from the *Holy Bible.* New Living Translation copyright© 1996, 2004, 2007 by Tyndale House Foundation. Used by permission of Tyndale House Publishers, Inc. Carol Stream, Illinois 60188. All rights reserved.

Scripture quotations marked AMPC are taken from the Amplified® Bible Classic Edition © 1954, 1958, 1962, 1964, 1965, 1987 by The Lockman Foundation, La Habra, CA 90631. All rights reserved.

Scripture quotations marked NCV are taken from the New Century Version of the Bible, copyright © 2005 by Thomas Nelson, Inc. Used by permission. All rights reserved.

Scripture quotations marked CEV are from the Contemporary English Version, Copyright © 1995 by American Bible Society. Used by permission.

Scripture quotations marked HCSB are taken from the Holman Christian Standard Bible ® Copyright © 1999, 2000, 2002, 2003, 2009 by Holman Bible Publishers. Used by permission.

Scripture quotations marked TLB are taken from the The Living Bible copyright © 1971 by Tyndale House Foundation. Used by permission of Tyndale House Publishers Inc., Carol Stream, Illinois 60188. All rights reserved.

Scripture quotations marked NLV are taken from the New Life Version copyright © 1969 and 2003. Used by permission of Barbour Publishing, Inc., Uhrichsville, Ohio 44683. All rights reserved.

Scripture quotations mared NIrV are taken from the Holy Bible, NEW INTERNATIONAL READER'S VERSION®. Copyright © 1195, 1996, 1998, 2014 by Biblica, Inc™. All rights reserved throughout the world. Used by permission of Biblica.

Published by Barbour Books, an imprint of Barbour Publishing, Inc., P.O. Box 719, Uhrichsville, Ohio 44683, www.barbourbooks.com

Our mission is to publish and distribute inspirational products offering exceptional value and biblical encouragement to the masses.

Member of the
Evangelical Christian
Publishers Association

Printed in China.

MORNING, EVENING. . . ALL DAY THROUGH

*The whole Bible was given to us by inspiration from God
and is useful to teach us what is true and to make us realize
what is wrong in our lives; it straightens us out and helps us
do what is right. It is God's way of making us well prepared
at every point, fully equipped to do good to everyone.*

2 TIMOTHY 3:16–17 TLB

This scripture verse from 2 Timothy helps you remember just how important the Bible is in your daily routine: It provides truthful instruction, strengthens your faith, and prepares you to live a godly life.

The *Bible Memory Plan for Morning & Evening* is a plan to help you grow closer to your heavenly Father through insightful devotional thoughts, prayers, and scriptures. As you begin and end each day with the Lord, you will find yourself more prepared for whatever life brings. Twice a day, for every day of the calendar year, meditate on the thoughts, say the prayers, and memorize each daily scripture. Carry the scripture verses with you. Repeat them until the words come easily. Then apply them to your daily life. Take note of how applying the verses transforms you, your relationships with others, and most importantly your relationship with God.

Allow God's Word to bless you as it becomes a part of who you are. . .

Be blessed, and be a blessing to others by sharing His Word.

MEMORY VERSE OF THE DAY

*"Be strong and of good courage; do not be afraid, nor be dismayed,
for the Lord your God is with you wherever you go."*

JOSHUA 1:9 NKJV

Morning

I AM STRONG.

God gives you strength and courage to face anything and everything. With Him, you can boldly go where no woman has gone before! Whenever fear creeps into your mind, say today's verse aloud and watch your doubts crumble before the presence of God!

*Thank You, Lord, for Your strength and encouragement.
With You at my side, I will not be afraid.*

Evening

I AM COURAGEOUS!

Nothing builds confidence more than knowing that God is in your corner when you step out into the world. Just have faith that He is with you, directing your day. Take courage. There's nothing you will face that He can't handle. Just do it!

Thank You, God, for giving me the courage to face any challenge that comes my way.

MEMORY VERSE OF THE DAY

Now all glory to God, who is able, through his mighty power at work within us, to accomplish infinitely more than we might ask or think.

Ephesians 3:20 nlt

Morning ———————————————————

I AM READY.

The things you can do when God is working through you are beyond your imagination, so don't limit yourself. Tap into His infinite power, connect to His Spirit, and let Him take the reins on your life. The results will be awesome!

God, I stand at the ready. Work through me!

Evening ———————————————————

FILL ME WITH YOUR GLORY!

The Lord wants you to come into His presence regularly, not in an "I have to get this over with" mindset, but with a "Lord, I am so blessed to get to spend time with You!" attitude. When you meet Him that way, His shining-greatness will be revealed, and He will fill you up with His glory.

I don't want to go through the motions, heavenly Father.
I want Your glory to fall upon me and Your shining—greatness to overwhelm me.

MEMORY VERSE OF THE DAY

"And when you are praying, do not use meaningless repetition as the Gentiles do, for they suppose that they will be heard for their many words."

MATTHEW 6:7 NASB

Morning

TEACH ME TO PRAY.

God does not judge your way with words. He knows your heart. He wants to hear from you. When you pray, first honor Him as Creator, Master, Savior, and Lord. Reflect on who He is and praise Him. Then confess and repent of your sins. Thank your heavenly Father, and make your requests known to Him.

Lord, Your Word says that my prayers rise up to heaven like incense from the earth. Remind me daily to send prayers Your way!

Evening

HELP ME TO BELIEVE.

The Lord enjoys pouring out blessing upon blessing. He enjoys the smile on your face when He says "Yes" to your requests. So don't be afraid to make your requests known. But when you pray, you must believe. Believe—such a small word, but such a big action.

Father, help me always to believe that You hear my prayers and that You will answer in a way that is best for me.

MEMORY VERSE OF THE DAY

*I have composed and quieted my soul; like a weaned child rests
against his mother, my soul is like a weaned child within me.*

PSALM 131:2 NASB

Morning

QUIET MY SOUL.

Do you sometimes feel like escaping from the world's wild ride? When things of
this world cannot satisfy you, remember that God can. Let Him wean you from
your daily worries. Like a small child, crawl up onto your heavenly Father's lap.
Breathe deeply. Relax in His presence and allow your soul to find rest.

*Father God, take me in Your arms. Hold me tight.
Fill me with Your comforting peace.*

Evening

I'M WEARY OF WORRY!

The key to a worry-free life is to accept the fact that you'll never have all the
answers—and that's okay. God knows everything, and He's got you covered. Just
trust Him. Rest in the knowledge that He has it all under control. All day, all night,
give your worries to Him.

*Lord, although I don't always understand why things happen,
I know I can rely on You.*

MEMORY VERSE OF THE DAY

*To everything there is a season,
a time for every purpose under heaven.*
ECCLESIASTES 3:1 NKJV

Morning

CHANGE HAPPENS.

There are seasons when everything falls into place and seasons when nothing appears to go right. Seasons change. But, with each change God gives you a fresh opportunity to recapture your hopes and dreams. You need only to open your heart, step out in faith, and trust Him.

*Dear God, when things change, for better or worse,
remind me to have faith and put all of my trust in You.*

Evening

ENCOURAGE ME!

There is so much about God and His blessings to focus on that you have no need to dwell on anything that brings you down. Still, sometimes, negative thoughts creep in. When that happens, remember that encouragement is always available by reading the Bible, praying, and meditating on God's words.

*Father God, help me to keep my mind fixed on You.
Sweep away any negative thoughts and encourage me with Your words.*

MEMORY VERSE OF THE DAY

For as he thinks within himself, so he is.

PROVERBS 23:7 NASB

Morning

WHO CARES WHAT *THEY* THINK!

Don't worry about what others think about you. Live your life to please God alone. He knows your heart. When you allow yourself to be real before Him, it doesn't matter what others think. If the God of the universe has accepted you, then who cares about someone else's opinion?

Dear Lord, may I live for You alone.
Help me transition from a people pleaser to a God pleaser.

Evening

LORD, GUIDE MY THOUGHTS.

Thoughts are powerful. What you believe within will appear without. Always stop and listen to the things you're telling yourself. If those thoughts and images are negative, renew your mind with thoughts from God's Word. Then watch your world transform.

Help me monitor my mind, Lord, and have thoughts pleasing to You.

MEMORY VERSE OF THE DAY

*The Lord is close to all who call on him, yes,
to all who call on him in truth.*

Psalm 145:18 nlt

Morning

GOD IS ALWAYS NEAR.

God's truth anchors your faith; and your faith gets His attention. God wants you to know He is nearby. He waits for you to grasp all that He has for you and to reap the blessings that come your way when you enter in to a trusting relationship with Him.

Dear Lord, help me to believe and trust that You are always near me.

Evening

I AM NEVER ALONE.

If you feel as if everyone in your life has scattered and left you, remember—God is with you. He will mend your broken heart, give you new purpose, and fulfill your desire for relationship. He understands loneliness and gently calls you to recognize His faithful, loving, and compassionate presence.

Thank You, God, for loving me so much that You never leave my side.

MEMORY VERSE OF THE DAY

A joyful heart is good medicine,
but a broken spirit dries up the bones.

PROVERBS 17:22 NASB

Morning

OH, HAPPY DAY!

Did you feel like crawling back into bed this morning? Wake up! God has something wonderful waiting for you. Joy. It works like medicine but has no negative side effects. Today, raise your hands to the sky, promise to be happy, and praise God for joy—even if you don't feel like it.

Father God, today help me to remember that You are the source of my joy.

Evening

PLEASE. RECHARGE ME.

Joyfulness might fade over time, for any number of reasons, but you know where to turn for a fresh start; God can renew your enthusiasm, recharge your batteries, and prod you to revisit your hopes and dreams. Trust Him and believe—He is the master at restoring lost joy.

Dear God, tonight as I sleep, please recharge my enthusiasm, passion, and joy.

MEMORY VERSE OF THE DAY

*"For I know the plans I have for you," declares the L*ORD,
*"plans to prosper you and not to harm you,
plans to give you hope and a future."*

JEREMIAH 29:11 NIV

Morning

GOD HAS A PLAN FOR ME.

Do you sometimes worry about finances and your future? Relax. God has a perfect plan for you. He has your life all worked out. Whew! Isn't that a relief? Unlike some of today's financial institutions, you can "bank" on God with absolute assurance. He promises you prosperity and fills your future with hope.

*I'm not sure what the future holds, Lord,
but I trust Your plans and await Your blessings.*

Evening

LORD, GIVE ME HOPE.

All hope is lost. What a negative thought that is! Whenever you feel hopeless, remember that God is the God of all hope. He is waiting to fill you up. Come to Him in prayer. Ask, believing, for hope, and prosperity. Before long, you'll be bubbling over with great expectations!

God of all hope, fill me to overflowing!

MEMORY VERSE OF THE DAY

For the LORD gives wisdom; from His mouth come knowledge and understanding. He stores up sound wisdom for the upright; He is a shield to those who walk in integrity, guarding the paths of justice, and He preserves the way of His godly ones.

PROVERBS 2:6–8 NASB

Morning

HELP ME GROW IN WISDOM.

God's Word says wisdom comes from the mouth of God, from the very words He speaks. The Bible was written through the inspiration of the Holy Spirit. Know that if you hold fast to the precepts in God's Word you will walk in integrity. Your feet will be planted on the straight and narrow road.

Lord, please give me the gift of Your guidance and help me to become wise through Your Word.

Evening

I WILL BUILD A FIRM FOUNDATION.

How can you provide guidance for your family without wisdom from the Lord? The Bible is God's blueprint for a godly home. When you memorize scripture, you set a firm foundation to build on. In order to strengthen your household, you must first seek God's wisdom through His holy Word.

Lord, You are the Master Builder. Help me to learn Your scripture so I can build a Godly home.

MEMORY VERSE OF THE DAY

"You did not choose me, but I chose you and appointed you that you should go and bear fruit and that your fruit should abide, so that whatever you ask the Father in my name, he may give it to you."
JOHN 15:16 ESV

Morning

YOU CHOSE *ME?!*

The Lord of all creation chose YOU! He saw you in your sinful state and said, "I'll take that one. I will adopt her and make her my own." Now, He longs for you to "bear fruit"—to lead by His example—so that you can guide others toward Him.

Father God, thank You for choosing me to be Your own.
Help me today to lead others to You.

Evening

I AM ONE OF GOD'S FAMILY.

You are one with millions of others around the globe who all have one important thing in common: They love God with all their hearts, souls, minds, and strength. We all belong to God and are beloved members of His family. So remember—gather with other believers to worship and pray together.

Dear heavenly Father, thank You for making me a member of Your family.

MEMORY VERSE OF THE DAY

Thank you for making me so wonderfully complex!
Your workmanship is marvelous—how well I know it.

PSALM 139:14 NLT

Morning

I AM PERFECTLY ME!

God thinks you are perfect just the way you are. He adores you, and He wants you to know just how much. On days when you're feeling down and need a boost of assurance, remember not only who you are—but *whose* you are. You belong to the King!

Father God, thank You for the fine job You did in making me.

Evening

PAMPERING IS ALLOWED.

Jesus is the King of kings. That makes you—a child of God—a princess! Embrace that sense of royalty and claim the privileges and power that come with it. You are royalty, so pamper yourself this Evening with a nice hot bath. Nothing buoys your spirit more than a tubful of water!

Thank You, Lord, for reminding me that I am worth some pampering.

MEMORY VERSE OF THE DAY

The heartfelt counsel of a friend is as sweet as perfume and incense.
PROVERBS 27:9 NLT

Morning

MY WORDS ARE IMPORTANT.

Words not only convey a message, they also reveal the attitude of your heart. Whether you are communicating with friends, family, or coworkers today, show that you value them. In all your conversations, extend God's grace to those hungry to experience His love. Be encouraging. Seek to build them up.

Dear Lord, may I view each conversation as an opportunity
to extend Your grace to others.

Evening

LET'S DO LUNCH.

Friendships that have Christ as their center are wonderful relationships blessed by the Father. Through the timely, godly advice these friends offer, God speaks to us, showering us with comfort that is as sweet as perfume and incense. So what are you waiting for? Make a date with a friend.

Jesus, thank You for my friends. Show me every day how to be
a blessing to them, just as they are to me.

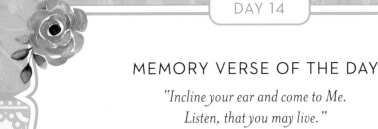

MEMORY VERSE OF THE DAY

"Incline your ear and come to Me.
Listen, that you may live."

Isaiah 55:3 nasb

Morning

MMM. . .LIFESAVERS.

God's Word is filled with lifesavers—life-saving scripture, that is. All you need to do is read His Word, listen for His message within the scriptures, and put His to-do plan into action. God's Word is sweeter than candy. And it's good to "eat" a little every day.

I'm opening myself up to You and Your Word, Lord.
Show me how to live!

Evening

I'M LISTENING, GOD.

Always keep your ears open to the sounds around you. Revel in knowing that God, as well as His creation, is speaking to you. All you need to do is stop—and listen. Listen attentively for God to speak to you. He'll let you know which way to go.

Speak to me, Lord! I'm listening! I want to hear Your voice.

MEMORY VERSE OF THE DAY

I call to God; God will help me. At dusk, dawn,
and noon I sigh deep sighs—he hears, he rescues.

PSALM 55:17 MSG

Morning

WAKE ME UP, JESUS!

Are you dragging this morning? Start your day with a cup of tea, or coffee, and Jesus. He is the best listener, and He can transform a sour mood into a cheerful one. A little time spent with Him can work wonders. Like no one else, Jesus can turn morning into cause for rejoicing.

Wake me up, Jesus! Light up my day with sunshine and joy.

Evening

LORD, HELP ME REST.

God wants you to relinquish your hold on time—or rather the hold time has on you. Lay down your ever-growing to-do lists. Right now commit your time to Him. Relax in His presence, knowing that He gives you all the time you need to do what is truly essential.

God, help me to set aside the cares of today and just rest here in Your love.

MEMORY VERSE OF THE DAY

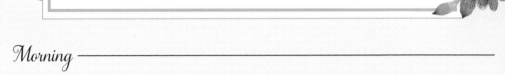

Sing to the Lord a new song; sing to the LORD, all the earth.

PSALM 96:1 NASB

Morning

I WILL SING TO THE LORD.

Start your day by singing to the Lord. Think about how rhythm is the heartbeat of a song. In giving us rhythm for our music and lives, our Creator has put His song in our hearts. May your song return to Him with a richness that brings honor to His glorious name.

Lord, I will sing to You a morning song with words of honor and praise.

Evening

I WILL BE STILL.

Take time tonight to be still and listen as God directs the wind to blow through the trees. Hear their branches sigh in mellow tones and the leaves whisper their chorus. No man-made music can compete with the music of nature. Praise God, right now, for His nighttime song.

Thank You, Father, for the kind of music that only You can perform.

MEMORY VERSE OF THE DAY

In him we live, and move, and have our being.

ACTS 17:28 KJV

Morning

IT'S A NEW DAY.

It's a new day in which God has given you breath and life. Relish the days He gives you. Take the opportunities He affords you. Cherish the love He has bestowed upon you and share it with others. Get out there, enjoy, and live this day to the fullest.

Lord, thank You for the gift of life and breath!

Evening

I NEED TO LET GO.

It's hard when you are working in your own power. What you need to recognize is the power of God's Spirit working within you. When you get attuned to the Spirit, He can do amazing things in, through, and with you. When you let go and let God, astonishing things happen.

Holy Spirit, I'm ready to step aside. Come shining through.

MEMORY VERSE OF THE DAY

"Don't you realize that I could ask my Father for thousands of angels to protect us, and he would send them instantly?"

MATTHEW 26:53 NLT

Morning

LORD, PROTECT ME.

Whenever you need protection you can breathe a huge sigh of relief because you have all the protection you need. God, Himself, protects you from anything evil. He intervenes, ready to take it on full-force. He is your defense. When you need help, speak His name. "Father God." He's there. Always.

Thank You, Father, for being my protection all the time wherever I go.

Evening

SEND ME SOME ANGELS.

If you knew that God's angels were standing in a circle around your bed would you sleep better? Relax! His angels are around you ready to protect at His command. Pull up the covers and get cozy. God's got all your worries, and He has plenty of angels to help.

God, I will sleep in peace knowing that You and Your angels are with me.

MEMORY VERSE OF THE DAY

Be careful to obey all these regulations I am giving you, so that it may always go well with you and your children after you, because you will be doing what is good and right in the eyes of the LORD your God.

DEUTERONOMY 12:28 NIV

Morning

GUIDE ME, LORD. TEACH ME.

When our children disobey, we feel disappointed and maybe sense that they don't love us. We think, if they did they would understand that our instructions are meant to guide them. This is how God feels when you fail to obey Him. He connects love with obedience. Do your best to obey Him today.

God, today and every day teach me and guide my steps.
Help me to obey You in all that I do.

Evening

FATHER, FORGIVE ME.

Confessing sin is part of obedience. When you admit to God that you've failed to obey Him, He can refresh your contrite heart and make You feel clean again. Think about today. Did You obey God all the time? Confess your sins to Him. Just as you forgive your own children, God will forgive you.

Lord forgive me for my sins and help me to do better—
thank You for loving me just as I am.

MEMORY VERSE OF THE DAY

*I pray that God, the source of hope, will fill you completely with joy
and peace because you trust in him. Then you will overflow with
confident hope through the power of the Holy Spirit.*

ROMANS 15:13 NLT

Morning

IT'S ALL ABOUT FAITH.

God wants to fill you to the brim with joy and peace. But to receive joy and peace,
you need to have faith in Him. Today, place your confidence in God who, in His
timing, will complete that task, mend that relationship, or do whatever else you
need.

Help me to grow in faith, God, knowing that You are the source of my joy.

Evening

GOD, DO YOU HEAR ME?

When your prayers remain unanswered, you should continue to pray. Even when
God is silent, you should continue to believe. When life turns you upside down,
when you ask, "Why?" God wants you to hold fast to your faith. He hears your
prayers, and He will answer them in His own time.

*Father, forgive me for allowing my problems to undermine my faith.
I trust in You. Help me to trust even more.*

MEMORY VERSE OF THE DAY

*Indeed, nothing in all creation will ever be able to
separate us from the love of God.*

ROMANS 8:39 NLT

Morning

YOU LOVE ME. YOU *REALLY* LOVE ME!

Some people shut God out because they feel ashamed of their sins. But you know better. In those times you need to cling to the assuring words in today's memory verse and be confident in God's unfailing, unconditional love. Nothing can separate you from His love—Nothing.

*I will not shut you out, God, because I know that you love me
all the time regardless of my sins.*

Evening

I'M *NOT* A FAILURE . . .

Whenever you fail, God offers a fresh start. He is always merciful and compassionate. When you fail, pick yourself up and hand that failure over to Him. When you trust in His love, you will learn not to be consumed by your failures. Your Father's compassion and mercy assures you of that.

*Thank You, Lord, for giving me a fresh start.
Build my confidence to keep on trying.*

MEMORY VERSE OF THE DAY

*But more than anything else, put God's work first
and do what he wants. Then the other things will be yours as well.*

MATTHEW 6:33 CEV

Morning

LORD, YOU'RE #1.

Your heavenly Father gives you opportunities to check your priorities. He puts you in situations where you have to choose between Him and your own desires. Putting yourself first brings frustration. Your work produces little progress. But when you put Him first, especially when you don't want to, He blesses you with joy.

*Father, I often forget to make You my priority. Help me today,
and every day, to put You first.*

Evening

BLESS ME, FATHER.

Joy comes when you put God first. Making Him your priority fills you with His love. He blesses you with peace and patience and teaches you kindness, goodness, faithfulness, gentleness, and to have self-control. The work His Holy Spirit does in you will change you and lead you toward pleasing God.

*Lord, bless me with peace, patience, kindness, goodness,
faithfulness, gentleness, and self-control.*

MEMORY VERSE OF THE DAY

Let the weak say, I am strong [a warrior]!

JOEL 3:10 AMPC

Morning

LOOK! I'M A WARRIOR!

As a child of God, you have amazing resources at your fingertips. One of those is His strength. You need not be a worrier when God has equipped you to be a warrior. Let "I am strong" be your battle cry today, then watch God help you to smash whatever gets in your way!

You are my stronghold, Lord! Victory is ours!

Evening

I CAN'T DO IT ALONE.

Trying to fight your battles alone can leave you feeling exhausted. Make God your partner, and let Him work through you. Remember—His Spirit has the power to do *anything*. So rest easy tonight. Trust God's Spirit to flow through you. Depend on Him to accomplish the impossible.

Work through me, Holy Spirit. I'm depending on You.

MEMORY VERSE OF THE DAY

Every good and perfect gift is from above, coming down from the Father of the heavenly lights, who does not change like shifting shadows.

JAMES 1:17 NIV

Morning

I WILL WATCH FOR BLESSINGS. . .

It's up to you to recognize the opportunities God has for you. Watch for His blessings. Listen to His direction and instruction so you can be quick to notice every good and perfect gift. God wants you to experience His favors and blessings, so expect Him to meet you at every turn.

Lord, thank You for setting favor and blessing in my path, and help me to expect it wherever I go, whatever I do.

Evening

I WILL WATCH FOR *YOU.*

Only one thing in your life will never change: Your heavenly Father. When things in the world shift and seem out of control, you can be certain that He is never surprised, never caught off guard by anything that happens. Watch for Him, and you will find Him in any difficulty.

Father, help me to watch for Your love and guidance when things seem out of control.

MEMORY VERSE OF THE DAY

I love those who love me, and those who seek me find me.

PROVERBS 8:17 NCV

Morning

WHERE ARE YOU, GOD?

When you seek God, you expect to find Him, but sometimes it's as if He's hiding. He might be holding back waiting for a change in your heart or He's speaking in a still, small voice, wanting you to be quiet and hear Him. Keep seeking. He's right there waiting for you to find Him.

Dear God, I'm listening. What do You need from me?
I want to feel close to You again.

Evening

GOD IS MY GPS.

Life's road is filled with detours. Sometimes it's hard to know which way to go. That's why it's critical to look for God's directions at every turn. He alone knows the right path for your journey. Lean on Him as your spiritual GPS. Wherever you need to go, He will get you there.

Lord, when I'm lost remind me to always rely on You for directions.

MEMORY VERSE OF THE DAY

My confusion is continually before me,
and the shame of my face hath covered me.

PSALM 44:15 KJV

Morning

CLUTTER, BE GONE!

The burdening clutter of negative thinking and bad choices keeps you from accomplishing what God wants you to do. Gather your clutter, relinquish it to Him, and allow Him to remove the burden from you. If spiritual clutter starts piling up again remember—you can repeat the process every day.

Heavenly Father, I don't want all this clutter in my life. Take it.
It's Yours. Help me to keep it from piling up again.

Evening

FORGIVE MY MESSY HEART.

With a mind unburdened of clutter, you can hear God speak. Go to Him as His child, unafraid, trusting Him to hold you in His arms. Tell Him about any messes you have made. Relish His fatherly love and forgiveness. It's in His arms that you will find peace.

Father, forgive me for my messy heart. Hold me gently in Your arms.
Love me, and give me peace.

MEMORY VERSE OF THE DAY

Those who say they live in God should live their lives as Jesus did.

1 JOHN 2:6 NLT

Morning

I WILL BE LIKE JESUS.

Much is said about superheroes these days, but the only true "superhero" is Jesus Christ who will never fail you. He alone was fully God and fully man. He alone possesses perfectly all the characteristics we most admire. Read about Him in God's Word and strive to be like Him.

Jesus, I want to be more like You.
Teach me through the Bible how to live a life like Yours.

Evening

I AM FOREVER FREE.

Thanks to Jesus, sin has no hold on you. When He died on the cross, Jesus took your sin away, freeing your soul from its bondage, so when you die you will be ready for eternal life in heaven. Jesus did this because He loves you. Believe it with all your heart.

Oh, Jesus, thank You so much for freeing my soul from sin.
I look forward to being with You in heaven someday.

MEMORY VERSE OF THE DAY

I have learned how to be content with whatever I have.

PHILIPPIANS 4:11 NLT

Morning

PLEASE, GIVE ME WHAT I NEED.

There's no good purpose in wishing for what you don't have. Instead, find delight in what you *do* have! God promises to provide for you. Tell Him what you want when you pray and trust Him to provide exactly what you need. He will not let you down.

As my Father, Lord, You have supplied me with all I need.
Thank You—for everything!

Evening

UNFRAZZLE ME.

Wishing and dreaming about what you don't have. It leads to frazzled, anxious feelings that disconnect you from the force that's yours for the taking—the power of God. Go to Him in prayer tonight. Rest in Him. Amid the quiet, meditate on His goodness and His desire to do what is best for you.

I come and rest in You, oh God,
confident that You will renew me with Your strength.

MEMORY VERSE OF THE DAY

Beloved, do not imitate what is evil, but what is good. The one who does good is of God; the one who does evil has not seen God.

3 JOHN 1:11 NASB

Morning ————————————————————

I WANT TO BE LIKE YOU.

As a child of God, His character is yours to imitate. The enemy entices you toward an "everyone does it" mindset. But as you immerse yourself in God's Word, you grow in knowledge through His sound teaching. When you apply the Truth of His Word you become more like Him.

Lord, teach me through Your scriptures and help me to apply them to my life.

Evening ————————————————————

HELP ME TO CHOOSE.

Life has many paths, and choosing a wrong one will hinder your growth toward God. Your heavenly Father gives you freedom of choice. But choose wisely. You can choose a path that leads to trouble or one that leads to Him. When in doubt, ask God to lead you.

When the choice isn't clear, Father,
please guide me to the right path—the one that leads to You.

MEMORY VERSE OF THE DAY

God has given each of you a gift from his great variety of spiritual gifts.

1 Peter 4:10 nlt

Morning

I AM *SO* TALENTED!

God has given you special gifts—things that you are good at— designed to be a blessing to others. Think about your God-given talents. Breathe new life into them. Allow them to shine, reflecting the love and glory of God. Use them to bless others—that's why God gave them to you.

Dear God, remind me of my God—given talents.
Help me to use them today to bless others.

Evening

I AM ABLE!

You may think that your talent isn't polished enough to share, but if God thought that, He wouldn't have given you His gifts. He trusts in your ability. He believes in you! Think about it: Who knows more about what you are capable of—you or God?

Lord, I want to share my God—given gifts.
Help me not to be shy, but to share Your gifts joyfully.

MEMORY VERSE OF THE DAY

Make this your common practice: Confess your sins to each other
and pray for each other so that you can live together whole and healed.

JAMES 5:16 MSG

Morning

THIS IS THE *REAL* ME.

Too often, we miss the value of sharing our failings. When you share your own experiences—especially your failures—you gain empathy, you're more approachable, and you increase your "relatability" to others. Let your guard down today and be who you are. Be the real you—flawed maybe, but someone striving to please God.

Lord, help me to be real with those You have put around me.
I pray that they see You through me and it draws them closer to You.

Evening

IT WAS MY FAULT.

Are you at fault? Are you to blame? Shame and fear might lead you to deny your shortcomings. If you worry about what God will think of you, remember this—He loves you flaws and all. You can always come into His presence to be forgiven and restored.

Thank You, Father, for Your cleansing love and for the joy I find in Your presence.

MEMORY VERSE OF THE DAY

*Our LORD and our God, you are like the sun and also
like a shield. You treat us with kindness and with honor,
never denying any good thing to those who live right.*

PSALM 84:11 CEV

Morning

FORGIVE ME. BLESS ME.

Aren't you glad that God doesn't stop the flow of blessings in your life when you
mess up? He bestows kindness and honor and doesn't withhold from those who
try to live right. Sure, you're not perfect, but as long as you ask for forgiveness for
your mess-ups, God's right there, ready to bless you.

*Thank You, God, for blessing me with honor and kindness,
even when I don't deserve it.*

Evening

I CAN COUNT ON GOD.

Jesus died for your sins and made you blameless. Because of that, God forgives
you, and you can count on His favor. You can also count on Him to shield you from
evil, because you need His protection to avoid going down the wrong path. Isn't it
wonderful that you can count on Him?

*I am so grateful, God, that I can always depend on You.
Help me to remember that in every situation.*

MEMORY VERSE OF THE DAY

*I focus on this one thing: Forgetting the past and
looking forward to what lies ahead.*

PHILIPPIANS 3:13 NLT

Morning

TODAY, I AM WHERE I SHOULD BE.

Wherever God has placed you today is exactly where you should be. Your job is to find out what you can do there to accomplish His purpose. Forget what happened yesterday. Focus instead on God. Ask Him to guide you, then watch His miracles unfold!

I thank You for where I am today, Lord. Show me what to do!

Evening

I WILL MOVE FORWARD.

There are days when past hurts and grievances hold you down from experiencing the life God has planned for you. Break free from those ties and fix your eyes on opportunities ahead. God has His plan for you all worked out. All you have to do is move forward!

*I'm cutting the ties that tie me to yesterday, Lord!
Help me to refocus on You and Your will for my life!*

MEMORY VERSE OF THE DAY

*And He said to them, "Come away by yourselves to a secluded place
and rest a while." (For there were many people coming and going,
and they did not even have time to eat.)*

MARK 6:31 NASB

Morning ————————————————————————

THERE'S BEAUTY ALL AROUND.

Take time today to stop and notice God's artistry: majestic mountains, plum and
brown with snowy white tops; streaks of red, yellow, and violet spread like fingers
in a sunrise or sunset; the deep blue ocean and the turquoise sea. God made all
creation—then He rested and admired His work.

*God, Your works are magnificent! Thank You—not only for them,
but also for reminding me to stop and take notice.*

Evening ————————————————————————

IT'S TIME TO RELAX.

We live in a nonstop society that urges us to rush in everything we do. But
sometimes God wants us to stop what we're doing and rest. After a period
of relaxation, the barrier of stress and fatigue eases. Objective views, logical
solutions, and creative ideas will flow again, refreshed and renewed.

*Father, I often forget how important it is to rest.
Clear my mind from all concerns, and bless me with a restful night's sleep.*

MEMORY VERSE OF THE DAY

"Therefore everyone who confesses Me before men,
I will also confess him before My Father who is in heaven."

MATTHEW 10:32 NASB

Morning

JESUS IS MINE!

Jesus came to earth as God in the flesh. God had tried to save us from sin by giving us His laws. He sent us His prophets, but people refused to listen. Finally, He sent His Son, Jesus, to save us so we will have eternal life in heaven. Oh, what a Savior you have in Him!

God, how good of You to love me so much that you sent me a Savior.
Hallelujah! Jesus is mine!

Evening

JESUS DEFENDS ME.

If you know Jesus Christ and have responded to His invitation to receive Him as Savior, then Jesus remains forever your advocate. Know that you are so precious to Jesus that He gave His life for you. Doesn't it feel incredible to have Jesus as your defender?

Jesus, how reassuring it is to know You mightily defend not only
my body but also my soul against attack.

MEMORY VERSE OF THE DAY

Taste and see that the LORD is good.
Oh, the joys of those who take refuge in him!
PSALM 34:8 NLT

Morning ─────────────────────────

I NEED COFFEE!

Are you a morning-coffee person? There's something about the smell of coffee brewing and that first taste that wakes you up and makes you ready for the day. Meet Jesus for coffee this morning. Talk with Him. Take pleasure in Him. Taste and see that the Lord is good!

Lord Jesus, come. Talk with me.
Provide me with all that I need to enter this day joyfully.

Evening ─────────────────────────

WARM MILK AT BEDTIME?

Some people think that a cup of warm milk helps them to sleep. The Bible tells us to long for the "pure milk of the word." God's Word is the best aid for a good night's rest. Get into the habit of reading the Bible at bedtime. Then sleep sheltered by God's love.

Father, Your Word is like the milk that calms a newborn child.
Lead me into the scriptures tonight, and soothe me with Your love.

MEMORY VERSE OF THE DAY

And my God will meet all your needs according to the riches of his glory in Christ Jesus.

PHILIPPIANS 4:19 NIV

Morning

GOD GIVES ME WHAT I NEED.

Aren't you glad that God is your ultimate supplier? When you're feeling depleted and when you don't think there's anything inside of you left to give, He supplies you with strength, courage, tenacity, and favor. He won't fail you. God will always come through as your supplier. That's a promise you can trust.

Dear God, thank You for meeting my needs with Your endless supply of mercy.

Evening

BUT WAITING IS HARD!

Have you ever felt as if God keeps you waiting? God rewards those who are diligent. If you're in a waiting season, don't give up. God hears your prayers, and He's going to come through in a big way. Praise Him instead of grumbling. It makes the wait much sweeter.

Lord, sometimes waiting is so difficult for me. Please help me with that. I love You, and I know that You will provide whatever I need.

MEMORY VERSE OF THE DAY

*I will ask the Father, and He will give you another Counselor
to be with you forever. He is the Spirit of truth.*

JOHN 14:16–17 HCSB

Morning ————————————————————————

THE HOLY SPIRIT IS MY HELPER.

We were not created to be alone. God made us social beings, dependent on one another, dependent on Him. Jesus sent the Holy Spirit to be your Helper. Ask and you can experience His comfort, counsel, and guidance immediately—right now. He is closer than you can ever imagine.

*Dear Jesus, send the Holy Spirit to guide me today.
Remind me throughout the day that my Helper is near.*

Evening ————————————————————————

I'M COMING UNDONE.

Are you overwhelmed? Coming undone? According to God's Word, you are an overcomer. Through the Holy Spirit, you have God-given strength to take on anything that robs you of your joy. God is greater than anything that can be thrown at you—and that gives you the breathing space you need to endure any situation.

*God, I'm coming undone. Put me back together.
Give me strength to endure through the Holy Spirit—my Helper.*

MEMORY VERSE OF THE DAY

*Because of Christ and our faith in him, we can now come boldly
and confidently into God's presence.*

EPHESIANS 3:12 NLT

Morning

LORD, GIVE ME CONFIDENCE.

Jesus walked in total God-confidence—knowing that His steps were planned. He had only to listen to His Father's heartbeat to know which way to go. Today, try living in total God-confidence, knowing that you'll be able to withstand anything life throws at you, because God is with you.

*Father, please give me all the confidence I need today
to overcome any obstacle in my path.*

Evening

TOMORROW IS A NEW DAY.

Maybe you started today feeling confident, but as the day went on your confidence waned. Don't beat yourself up if you didn't meet your own expectations. Tomorrow is another of God's wonderful gifts. He gives you the opportunity to try again. So, put today away. Rest now in His never-ending love.

*I can be so hard on myself sometimes. God, please remind me that I'm not perfect—
and that's okay. Tomorrow is a new day full of possibilities.*

MEMORY VERSE OF THE DAY

*But those who hope in the LORD will renew their strength.
They will soar on wings like eagles; they will run and
not grow weary, they will walk and not be faint.*

Isaiah 40:31 NIV

Morning ————————————————————————

GOD HOLDS MY HAND.

Life can sometimes feel like you're at the edge of a cliff and about to fall off.
Remember—God is the only constant, the only One who without a doubt can
shield you from trouble. He will always lift you up. Put your hand in His, and you
won't fall.

*Lord, You are my safe haven.
As I abide in You today, fill me with Your strength.*

Evening ————————————————————————

I WILL FLY!

The Bible says that those who hope in the Lord will soar high on wings like eagles.
So, whenever you stand at the edge of a life-cliff, ask God to help you. Fly! Put on
your wings of hope and take off with God-given strength. He will help you to soar
above your troubles.

*Father, help me not to be afraid. Give me the strength to rise above my problems,
knowing that You have everything under control.*

MEMORY VERSE OF THE DAY

The Lord God is my strength, and He has made my feet like hinds' feet,
and makes me walk on my high places.

HABAKKUK 3:19 NASB

Morning

WHAT IF I STUMBLE?

Your heavenly Father frees you from dread of danger as you scale the rugged terrain of your life. You can hike a trail of uncertainty with confidence knowing God is with you. If you stumble, in His mercy He will pick you up, strengthen you, and set you back on your feet.

Lord, as long as I hold tight to Your hand,
I know that I won't stumble through life.
I will put my trust in You.

Evening

AND IF I LOSE FAITH?

You will encounter traffic jams in your faith—times when worldly cares pile up and seem to separate you from God. When this happens, the Bible says you should wait patiently for the Lord's help. He will provide truth and wisdom to show you how to get your faith flowing again.

Dear Lord, I don't want worldly cares to separate me from You.
Come to me. Build up my faith.

MEMORY VERSE OF THE DAY

Do not merely listen to the word,
and so deceive yourselves. Do what it says.

JAMES 1:22 NIV

Morning

I WILL LIVE GOD'S WORD.

We're promised in the Word of God that we are capable of sticking with it. We can read the Word of God, absorb the Word of God, and live the Word of God. It's doable. And this heavenly "sticktoitiveness" means we can see each project—and each challenge—from start to finish.

Heavenly Father, the Bible has all that I need to meet any challenge.
Help me to absorb Your word and to live by it.

Evening

GOD IS MY TEACHER.

As you memorize and apply the scriptures in this book, God teaches you to become more like Jesus. He leads you to apply His Word to your work, your relationships, and to every challenge you face. Don't just read the Bible. Think about its words. What have you learned from them today?

God, teach me! Help me to focus on Your words
and allow them to soak deep into my soul.

MEMORY VERSE OF THE DAY

Then young women will dance and be glad, young men and old
as well. I will turn their mourning into gladness;
I will give them comfort and joy instead of sorrow.

JEREMIAH 31:13 NIV

Morning

GOD TURNS SAD HEARTS GLAD.

Don't you love this promise in today's scripture verse? God can turn a sad heart glad! This joy comes as a free gift. You don't have to earn it. You don't have to beg for it. Just reach out and grab it, then watch as you are strengthened for the days ahead.

Thank You, God, for the promise of gladness.

Evening

MY HEART BELONGS TO HIM.

Can you see how God uses everything, even your pains and your hurts, to build your character and draw you closer to Him? Whatever you're going through right now—this very moment—rest assured, God will work it for your good, as long as your heart belongs to Him.

Father God, my heart belongs to You. Come and live within me.
Fill my heart with Your love.

MEMORY VERSE OF THE DAY

My soul, wait thou only upon God; for my expectation is from him.
PSALM 62:5 KJV

Morning ————————————————————

I CAN EXPECT GOOD THINGS.

The one thing you can count on is God. Simply have patience, confident He will do as promised. Go out today with assurance, expecting good things from the Lord; in doing so, you'll find your cup runneth over!

I wait upon You only, God.
My hands are open, waiting to receive!

Evening ————————————————————

I BELIEVE.

Did you exercise your faith today? Did you believe that, regardless of what you observed in the material world, God was, and is, working on your behalf? There's no doubt about it; God is working in unseen ways to bring good things into your life. Blessed are those who believe!

Lord, You are working in my life,
giving it substance. And I praise You for it!

MEMORY VERSE OF THE DAY

You died to this life, and your real life is hidden with Christ in God.
COLOSSIANS 3:3 NLT

Morning

WHAT IF I ONLY SEE SCARS?

You may wish that you could hide the scars in the picture of your life. But those impressions have meaning and purpose; everything you see as a scar is evidence of a wound that God has healed. When you look at your life, you only see the blemishes. But God sees your beauty.

My loving Father, thank You for seeing the beauty in me.
Help me to see it, too.

Evening

OUT WITH THE OLD!

The minute you accepted Christ as your Savior, your old life with all its battle scars passed into oblivion. God gave you a new life in Him. He sees your goodness and your potential, but it's up to you to believe and work at being the best that you can be.

God, help me to recognize and then build on all the goodness and potential within me.

MEMORY VERSE OF THE DAY

*Let no corrupt communication proceed out of your mouth,
but that which is good to the use of edifying, that it may
minister grace unto the hearers.*

EPHESIANS 4:29 KJV

Morning

MY WORDS WILL HONOR GOD. . .

Imagine if a filter were placed over your mouth to capture all your distasteful words. How dirty would that filter become? God wants your words to be soothing and inspiring, never bitter or distasteful. Ask Him to help with your words today. Use them to bring God's message of love to those around you.

*Heavenly Father, forgive my harsh and bitter words. Help me to filter
my speech so I may bring comfort and joy to others.*

Evening

. . .EVEN WHEN I'M ANGRY.

Before you allow angry words to hurt someone, pause. Go to a quiet place to get alone with God. Ask Him to control the situation. In the heat of an angry moment, give your anger to Him, and He'll prepare your heart to deal with the situation the way He wants you to.

*Lord, enable me to trust You wholly with my anger
and keep me from sinning with my words.*

MEMORY VERSE OF THE DAY

The LORD is King forever and ever;
nations have perished from His land.

PSALM 10:16 NASB

Morning

JESUS IS KING—NOW AND FOREVER!

Satan devotes all his efforts to eradicating Christianity. His influence is ugly, but it will not be permanent. The reason? God's Son, Jesus, lives forever within those who call upon His name. He is and will remain King and will one day come back to claim this earth for His own, forever and ever.

Lord, as this world becomes increasingly evil, remind me that
You're coming back to claim all that is rightfully Yours.

Evening

I WILL BE WATCHFUL.

Keep your eyes open. Watch. Satan roams the earth putting obstacles in your way. Don't let them stop you; that's exactly what he wants. Rely on Jesus, Your Great King, to destroy anything that gets in the way of you living the joyful and godly life that He wants you to have.

Jesus, help me, please, to be watchful and rely on You to keep me
from falling into Satan's traps.

MEMORY VERSE OF THE DAY

I will instruct you and teach you in the way you should go.

PSALM 32:8 NIV

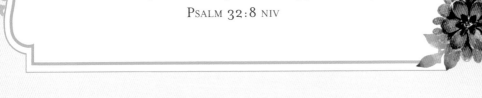

Morning

HE SHOWS ME THE WAY.

God knows which way you should go. You need to play your part, of course, seeking His guidance, listening for it, and then following it. Knowing that it is God who has pointed you in a certain direction can give you peace of mind and confidence in the decisions you make.

*Father, show me the way. teach me to seek Your guidance
and to make the right decisions.*

Evening

GOD LISTENS TO ME.

God listens to Your most intimate thoughts. He not only listens but also answers your pleas and guides you in every way. You can be assured that your God, the God of endless love and compassion, will always give you His full attention. Talk with Him tonight. He's listening.

Heavenly Father, hear my prayer. I have much to tell You tonight. . .

MEMORY VERSE OF THE DAY

Whoever gives heed to instruction prospers,
and blessed is the one who trusts in the LORD.

PROVERBS 16:20 NIV

Morning

IF I READ THE INSTRUCTIONS. . .

Do you read directions, or do you jump right in and try to do it all on your own? Sometimes, only when we fail, do we read the instructions. Before walking out the door this morning, find inspiration and instruction from scripture. Then trust in God's guidance, and you will prosper as promised!

Thank You, Lord, for Your Guidebook and helping me to walk Your way.

Evening

IT'S ALL IN THE BOOK.

Whenever you feel lost or unsure about how to approach a situation, remember— all of the answers are in The Book. The Bible holds instructions for everything. Become familiar with the Word of God. As you read it, ask God to lead you. Read expecting to find exactly what you are looking for.

Dear God, I need answers. Open my mind and heart as I read Your Word.
Lead me in the right direction.

DAY 50

MEMORY VERSE OF THE DAY

Be joyful in hope, patient in affliction, faithful in prayer.
ROMANS 12:12 NIV

Morning

I NEED A BOOST!

Sometimes, even a sunny morning isn't enough to send you joyfully into the day. Solar energy is the new green. But it's got nothing on God, the mightiest power source you have. Need recharging? Put your hope in God. Plug into His promises. He'll give you strength to get through the day.

Lord, I need a boost of energy. Fill me with Your power
so that I can have a productive day.

Evening

I NEED TO SLOW DOWN.

A boost of energy is great to begin the day, but if that energy keeps going. . .and going. . .and going into the night, you know what happens—you can't sleep! God can help with that, too. Quiet yourself with thoughts of His love. Trust Him to soothe you and help you to sleep.

Father God, thank You for loving me gently and quieting my soul.
Lead me now to restful sleep.

MEMORY VERSE OF THE DAY

*Satisfy us in the morning with your unfailing love,
that we may sing for joy and be glad all our days.*
PSALM 90:14 NIV

Morning

I AM SATISFIED.

What joy, to live a satisfied life. No cravings. No longings. No "what ifs." Just a blissful state of realizing that all you could ever want is right in front of you. And it is, you know, because God is right there, totally in control, meeting your every need.

Heavenly Father, You satisfy all my needs, every day, all day. Thank You!

Evening

GOD'S GOT IT!

Tonight, put aside any problem that bothers you. You needn't worry because God's got it! He's got it under control. You might not see a change in your situation, but you can find comfort in knowing that God already has it all worked out. Be patient. Rest in His love and trust Him.

*God, I trust in Your unfailing love. I will be satisfied knowing
that You have my problems all worked out.*

MEMORY VERSE OF THE DAY

Two people are better off than one,
for they can help each other succeed.

ECCLESIASTES 4:9 NLT

 Morning

FRIENDS AT WORK. . .

Solitary work is sometimes necessary, but too much solitude can lead to sluggishness and dull ideas. God provides us with friends at work to help us not only get the job done, but also to succeed. Seek out God-loving friends at work. Team up with them and rely on each other for help.

Lord, lead me to friends at work who love You as I do.
Two, or more, are better than one!

Evening

FRIENDS AT PLAY.

The Bible warns about choosing friends carefully so you won't be led astray. A night out with friends is fun, but be careful that how you play is still pleasing to God. Be wise about the friends you choose. God-given friends will strengthen your bond with Him and not lead you astray.

Heavenly Father, guide me to choose my friends wisely,
and help us to please You with all that we do.

MEMORY VERSE OF THE DAY

"Truly I tell you, if anyone says to this mountain, 'Go, throw yourself into the sea,' and does not doubt in their heart but believes that what they say will happen, it will be done for them."

MARK 11:23 NIV

Morning

MY FAITH CAN MOVE MOUNTAINS.

When faced with an obstacle that won't budge, put on your faith glasses and see it through God's eyes. Then, with all of the confidence you can muster, holler to that mountain, "Hey, you! Get out of here!" Might sound childish, but that kind of faith could just clear the road in front of you!

Lord, by putting my faith in You, nothing will get in my way. I have faith, Lord—but, please, give me more.

Evening

WHEN IS IT GOOD TO BE CHILDISH?

Young children have faith in things unseen. And that is how God wants you to be. You are His child, and He wants you to have complete faith in His ability to lead and protect you in every circumstance. Allow yourself to be vulnerable with Him. Rely on Him for all your needs.

Father God, I come before You as a little child, wanting and needing You in every way. Guide me, Lord, and protect me.

MEMORY VERSE OF THE DAY

Do not neglect to show hospitality to strangers,
for by this some have entertained angels without knowing it.

HEBREWS 13:2 NASB

Morning ————————————————————

I MIGHT MEET AN ANGEL.

God calls us to help in precarious situations. When you help a stranger, or let one assist you, you won't know if the stranger is an angel, or if the presumed angel is a mere human—but God knows. Listen to your heart and be watchful. God might ask you to help a stranger today.

Dear God, today, I will watch for someone in need
and listen for Your guidance. Show me how I can help.

Evening ————————————————————

LET ME ENTERTAIN YOU.

Jesus often relied on the hospitality of strangers for a hot meal and a place to stay. This shows that God wants us to welcome others into our lives and homes. Maybe there is a new family in your church or neighborhood. How about inviting them over for a meal and some fun?

Jesus, help me to open my heart and home to new friends.
Guide me in showing them some welcoming hospitality.

MEMORY VERSE OF THE DAY

"Blessed are those who mourn, for they shall be comforted."
MATTHEW 5:4 NASB

Morning

I WILL MEET SADNESS HEAD–ON.

No one escapes sadness. God knows that grieving alone can deepen the sorrow, so He puts friends and family members in people's lives to comfort them. It is His blessing. You can show the love of Christ when you sit with grieving friends and let them talk, or let them cry, or cry with them.

Lord, sometimes I shy away from sadness. Teach me to be a comfort to those who are mourning. Show me how I can help.

Evening

GOD IS MY COMFORT.

You can rely on God's love in times of sadness. He is the Great Comforter. When nothing else can bring you any consolation, God will wipe away the tears from your eyes. There will no longer be any mourning, crying, or heartfelt pain when you put your trust in His healing love.

Dear God, I believe that You can heal my broken heart. Come to me, please, and be my Comfort.

MEMORY VERSE OF THE DAY

The LORD came and stood there, calling as at the other times,
"Samuel! Samuel!" Then Samuel said,
"Speak, for your servant is listening."

1 SAMUEL 3:10 NIV

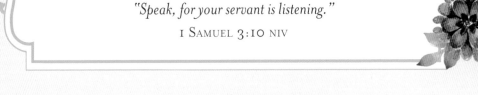

Morning

SPEAK, LORD. I'M LISTENING.

God speaks powerfully through His Word, the Bible, and also whispers truth to our hearts. He most often communicates to servant hearts that are ready to listen—hearts committed to obedience. Is your heart receptive to His call today? Work toward being able to say sincerely, "Speak, Lord, Your servant is listening!"

Dear Lord, bless me with a servant's heart,
a heart committed to obedience.

Evening

I WILL HEAR YOUR VOICE.

Do your prayers seem to hit the ceiling and bounce back? Is God's voice distant, or not at all? Trust that God hears you. Believe that He will respond. All He asks is that your reliance on Him remains firm. At just the right time, He will speak in your heart.

Father, I trust that You hear me—now, please, let me hear Your voice.

MEMORY VERSE OF THE DAY

God decided in advance to adopt us into his own family by bringing us to himself through Jesus Christ. This is what he wanted to do, and it gave him great pleasure.

EPHESIANS 1:5 NLT

Morning

I AM GOD'S CHILD.

That day when God ushered you into His family, all of the promises in His Word became yours. God received great pleasure from adopting you as His own. What joy to be included in His eternal family! You can't help but celebrate that your Heavenly Father chose you.

Heavenly Father, thank You for choosing me to be Your child.
Knowing I am Yours fills my heart with joy.

Evening

THANK GOD FOR EVERYTHING!

The promise of eternal life in heaven is the greatest gift you will ever receive. Thank God, over and over, for this precious gift. And when you pray, remember to praise God for *everything* He gives you. Take time tonight to meditate on all that you forget to thank Him for. Then—give thanks.

Lord, thank You for everything, especially those little things that I so often forget.

MEMORY VERSE OF THE DAY

"Ask, and it will be given to you; seek, and you will find;
knock, and it will be opened to you."

MATTHEW 7:7 NASB

Morning

COME ON IN.

Are you looking for direction? Do you need help with a problem? God's door is always open. He'll give you the answers, help you find what you're looking for, and provide you with opportunities when you knock. Don't just sit there! Come on in. The Lord is waiting for you.

Father God, here I am—asking, seeking, knocking.

Evening

DOUBT? NOT ME!

Doubt does not fit with prayer. It's one thing to pray for something. It's another to believe you'll get it. Once you ask, trust that God will bring it to pass. Do not waver. Do not doubt. Keep your heart and mind united, and God will turn your requests into reality.

Lord, I believe! My heart and mind are one.

MEMORY VERSE OF THE DAY

"I know that you can do all things;
no purpose of yours can be thwarted."

JOB 42:2 NIV

Morning

BUT, WHY?

Sometimes what you think should happen, doesn't. But rest assured, God has a great plan for your life. All you need to do is be patient and let Him work it out. He can turn ashes into beauty. What a wonderful God you have! Expect good things from Him today.

I have so many "whys" Lord, but I believe that You will somehow
work everything out for my good. Thank You.

Evening

I CAN REST ASSURED.

Thinking about and worrying over "whys" can make you feel exhausted, grumpy, and overwhelmed. Perhaps it's time to be still. Rest, and rest assured that God is at work on your "whys." After a good night's sleep, you will rise with a calmer heart and mind, refreshed and renewed.

Lord, hold me in Your arms as I rest in You.

MEMORY VERSE OF THE DAY

Be strong in the Lord and in his mighty power.
Ephesians 6:10 NIV

Morning

GOD IS MY POWER SOURCE.

Meditate on this today: God is like the wind, a powerful, unseen force that lifts you above your circumstances and enables you to dance amid your difficulties. He is the power and energy that gives you strength to carry on, in every way, despite any opposing force that tempts you to quit.

Lord, like leaves on the wind,
lift me up and let me dance above the storm.

Evening

HE IS EVER PRESENT.

Like the wind, God is invisible, yet you can see evidence of His impact on your life. At times, you may wonder if He is still working on your behalf. But then you will sense that gentle nudge—or that strong gale—and you have all the evidence you need.

Dear God, thank You for providing evidence that You are always with me.

MEMORY VERSE OF THE DAY

The Lord is good, a strong refuge when trouble comes.

NAHUM 1:7 NLT

Morning

I NEED THE RAIN.

When rain falls on your life, you might not always experience it as something refreshing. But there is good reason to rejoice in the rain. Why? Because the seeds God planted in you, possibly many seasons earlier, need gentle rain for steady growth—and occasional storms for strengthening growth.

Father, when rain comes into my life, remind me to rejoice knowing that You are working to strengthen me.

Evening

I WILL BE SOMEONE'S SUNSHINE.

By allowing rainy days—those tough times—into your life, the Lord may be leading you into a mission to help others. What you learn on those dark days, God wants you to share. Meditate on this awhile: How can the life lessons you learned on your darkest days bring sunshine into someone's life?

The lessons might have been hard, Lord, but now I can use what I've learned to help others. Guide me. Show me what to do.

MEMORY VERSE OF THE DAY

*The fear of the LORD prolongs life,
but the years of the wicked will be shortened.*

PROVERBS 10:27 NASB

Morning

I WILL LEAD MY CHILDREN TO YOU.

Instead of being a cause of terror in your heart, the phrase "fear of the Lord" means to reverence and honor Him as your God. He alone is God, righteous and wise enough to intervene and effect positive changes in your life. Instilling this truth in your children enables them to know His ways.

God, I will teach my children to honor You. I will instruct them in Your ways.

Evening

HOPE FLOODS MY LIFE.

God's very nature is goodness. Therefore, everything that stems from Him reflects His character. This knowledge should cause hope to flood your life. Unshaken by the winds of change, you can stand firm in the face of any kind of adversity, like a boat anchored to its strong moorings.

*Thank You, dear Lord, for Your never—ending goodness.
Thank You for giving me hope.*

MEMORY VERSE OF THE DAY

God is faithful, who has called you into fellowship with his Son, Jesus Christ our Lord.

1 CORINTHIANS 1:9 NIV

Morning

JESUS IS MY COMPANION.

Today's scripture holds an amazing promise: God has called you to fellowship (to have companionship) with His Son, Jesus. Your Savior is with you, ready to dry your tears and give you strength and courage to put one foot in front of the other. Jesus is your companion. Wow! What a blessed privilege.

Jesus, how wonderful that You are my constant companion!
I love it that You are my dearest Friend.

Evening

MY LIFE IS BUILT ON PROMISES.

By now, you might have noticed that God's Word holds many promises. These truths are meant for you and everyone who believes. As you memorize scripture, God's promises become the foundation of your life. Rely on His Word. Each promise is like an indestructible rock that stands the test of time.

Father, help me to commit Your promises to memory and to trust them every day.

MEMORY VERSE OF THE DAY

*"You are the salt of the earth. But if the salt loses its saltiness,
how can it be made salty again? It is no longer good for anything,
except to be thrown out and trampled underfoot."*

MATTHEW 5:13 NIV

Morning ——————————————

I CAN LIVE A SALTY LIFE!

What a wonderful promise from God that you can be "salt" for those whose lives
are bland without Him. Your daily routine might seem mundane to you, but others
are watching and learning from your dedication to the Lord, family, and friends.
Their lives are being flavored by your faithfulness.

*Dear God, help me always to present a good example
of what it means to lead a godly life.*

Evening ——————————————

WHAT IF MY SALT RUNS OUT?

No one is perfect. We all have times when we don't present a godly example
for others. When that happens, don't give up. When you give up you lose your
saltiness—your positive impact on the lives of others. Ask God to refill your
saltshaker tonight. He will be happy to do it!

Heavenly Father, replenish my supply of salt. Then help me to use it wisely.

MEMORY VERSE OF THE DAY

We know that in all things God works for the good of those who love him.
ROMANS 8:28 NIV

Morning

I'M ABOUT TO BOIL OVER!

Sometimes, in the heat of things, your angry emotions might spill over. You won't make a good impression if that happens. God knows when you're near your boiling point, and He is there to help. When anger rises up inside you, focus on Him, and He will keep you in check.

Father God, when anger overwhelms me,
remind me to stop and allow You to control my emotions.

Evening

WHAT A MESS.

If you do boil over, and make a mess, remember this: God will help you to clean it up. There is simply no mess too big for Him. He is quick to forgive and restore. Put your faith in Him, and He will take Your mess and make it into something good.

Oh, Lord, I've made a mess of things! Forgive me. Take what I've done.
Turn it into something that gives You the glory.

MEMORY VERSE OF THE DAY

In the day of trouble he will keep me safe in his dwelling.

PSALM 27:5 NIV

Morning

DANGER! DANGER!

There are many dangers in this world, and you cannot escape them unless you are in God's safe house. Where He dwells, nothing can ever truly harm you. When you run to Him, He opens the door to you, spreading His protective arms to cover you. God is always there, waiting.

Heavenly Father, when storms rage I find comfort knowing
there is a safe haven ahead.

Evening

WHERE IS GOD'S SAFE HOUSE?

When you were a child, you knew you could run home when you were frightened. Just as children seek the safety of a loving home, you need a place to feel safe. So, where is God's safe house? In your heart where He lives. Run there. Pray. Allow Him to comfort and calm you.

Whenever I feel afraid, Lord, I will remember that You are there inside my heart,
just waiting for me to run home.

MEMORY VERSE OF THE DAY

No, dear brothers and sisters, I have not achieved it, but I focus on this one thing: Forgetting the past and looking forward to what lies ahead.

PHILIPPIANS 3:13 NLT

Morning

FORWARD, MARCH . . .

Try walking forward while looking behind you. You can't do it without stumbling, right? Now walk facing forward and pay attention to what's around you. A new opportunity lies ahead. So, instead of lamenting past decisions, hurts, and failures, move forward knowing that God is leading you to greater opportunities.

Lord, help me move forward, knowing You are with me every step of the way. Better days await me!

Evening

WITH A NEW ATTITUDE!

Are you ready to replace your worldly negatives with spiritual positives? Then, tonight, pull yourself away from the TV and snuggle up with the Bible. By reading God's Word, you will find your mind refreshed and your spirit lifted so you can move forward with a confident new attitude.

Fill my mind with the goodness of Your Word, Lord. Keep my heart, mind, soul, and spirit focused on You as I step out into the world.

MEMORY VERSE OF THE DAY

Let us test and examine our ways, and return to the Lord!
LAMENTATIONS 3:40 ESV

Morning

I WILL EXAMINE MY WAYS.

Take time today to examine your lifestyle. Is it pleasing to the Lord, or does it separate you from Him? The Holy Spirit will gently show you your sins, if you ask. Confess them to God so you may experience His forgiveness and your fellowship with Him can be restored.

*God, help me to be willing to examine my ways. Speak to me,
through Your Holy Spirit, of what is wrong in my life.*

Evening

AM I TOO BUSY FOR GOD?

What if you could follow yourself around for the day, carefully examining all that you do? Maybe your heart desires intimacy with God, but a real day in your life leaves no time. God often speaks to us in the stillness and silent spaces. How will you hear Him if you're never still?

*Lord, help me to still myself before You. Give me the gift of repentance
and allow me to enjoy the sweetness of Your forgiveness.*

MEMORY VERSE OF THE DAY

How can a young person stay on the path of purity?
By living according to your word.

PSALM 119:9 NIV

Morning ———————————————

GOD'S WORD IN THE MORNING. . .

The Bible contains true stories of kingdoms, journeys, wars, and love—sixty-six small books, all of them tied together. It begins with the creation of a perfect world, follows the world through its downfall, and ends victoriously with everything restored. Start each day with God's Word. Allow its truths to lead you.

Lord, lead me into the day with Your Word.
Keep it in my heart all day through.

Evening ———————————————

GOD'S WORD AT NIGHT.

As you read the Bible, think of it as a how-to on living a pure life. It educates us in politics, health issues, and Middle-eastern cultures. It's a mystery, dropping clues to what will come in the future, and a thriller with good repeatedly overcoming evil. Read it tonight, and discover something new.

Heavenly Father, speak to me through Your Word tonight.
What will You teach me?

MEMORY VERSE OF THE DAY

He saith unto them, Follow me, and I will make you fishers of men.

MATTHEW 4:19 KJV

Morning ————————————————————————

GO, FISH!

Jesus called Simon Peter and his brother, Andrew, into His ministry because they knew how to catch fish. Today, Jesus calls you to do just what Peter and Andrew did—cast your net with the love of Christ and draw in new believers for the Kingdom of God. Make that your mission today.

*Jesus, today I will make it a priority to tell others about You
and invite them to enter God's kingdom.*

Evening ————————————————————————

FISHING REQUIRES PATIENCE.

Maybe you tried to share God's Word with someone today, you cast your net , and it came back empty. Don't give up! Check your fishing methods. The Lord's solution requires care and perseverance. Listen to His nudging. When you trust and obey Him, He will fill your net with abundance.

*Lord, teach me how to lead others to You.
Give me the right words at just the right time.*

MEMORY VERSE OF THE DAY

"Martha, Martha," the Lord answered,
"you are worried and upset about many things."

LUKE 10:41 NIV

Morning

MARTHA, MARTHA, MARTHA!

When Jesus visited His friends, Mary and Martha, He reprimanded Martha for being too busy. Mary spent all her time with Jesus listening to His wisdom, but Martha was more concerned about being a good hostess and the preparations she had to make. Be like Mary today. Make Jesus your priority.

Jesus, forgive me for being too distracted by worldly issues to spend time with You. Here I am, Lord, ready to listen.

Evening

THE WORLD'S GOT ME DOWN.

It's easy these days to be worried and upset. Our world is unsettled. Life moves at break-neck speed, racing toward something—but, what? Instead of worrying about worldly cares, run to the One who is always in control, the One who waits with open arms. Run, right now, to Jesus.

Dear Savior, tonight I will set aside all of my worries and rest, safe in Your loving arms.

MEMORY VERSE OF THE DAY

For the word of God is alive and active. Sharper than any double—edged sword, it penetrates even to dividing soul and spirit, joints and marrow; it judges the thoughts and attitudes of the heart.

HEBREWS 4:12 NIV

Morning

THERE IS POWER IN GOD'S WORD.

Have you memorized each day's scripture? If not, don't give up. Start again with today's verse. Each scripture you memorize is like a weapon against evil. When life turns you upside-down, you can right yourself with God's Word. Whenever you apply it to your life, you release His mighty power.

Father, sometimes I get busy and forget to store Your Word in my heart. I will try to do better.

Evening

GOD'S WORD IS MY SHIELD.

God's Word serves as a sturdy shield when Satan flings arrows your way. Stand tall in faith. Repel those arrows with scripture. The Bible is the best weapon you have against the enemy. Stock up on its verses. Be sure that your quiver is full so you are prepared for a surprise attack.

Lord, arm me with Your words. Teach me to use them for every good purpose.

MEMORY VERSE OF THE DAY

Know therefore that the LORD your God is God; he is the faithful God,
keeping his covenant of love to a thousand generations of those
who love him and keep his commandments.

DEUTERONOMY 7:9 NIV

Morning

HE NEVER LETS ME DOWN.

God is always true to His Word. If He says it, He will do it. He won't ever let you down. Your Father agrees never to leave or forsake you. Did you hear that? *Never!* That's a promise you can genuinely trust. He says it and He will do it.

Dear God, thank You for Your eternal faithfulness.
Thank you for never letting me down.

Evening

HE MEETS ALL MY NEEDS.

When you seek God, then He will graciously provide all that you need. If you remember this, you don't have to fret about anything—your provision, your strength, anything! God knows what you need at this very moment and throughout your life. He holds it, all ready, in the palm of His hand.

Heavenly Father, You know better than I what I really need,
so I won't worry. You will provide!

MEMORY VERSE OF THE DAY

A man who endures trials is blessed, because when he passes the test he will receive the crown of life that God has promised to those who love Him.

JAMES 1:12 HCSB

Morning

IF AT FIRST I DON'T SUCCEED. . .

How do you handle difficulties? Do the words "I'm not good enough" play through your head? God says that you ARE good enough. He gives you the power to endure your challenges and to keep on trying. A positive attitude plus endurance equals success. Remember that with every challenge you meet today.

Dear Lord, I will keep my eyes fixed on You and keep moving forward, regardless of what happens today.

Evening

I WILL TRY, TRY AGAIN.

God calls for perseverance more than a dozen times in the New Testament. He permits trials to enter your life to increase your strength. When you successfully pass small hurdles, He may let even bigger ones stand in your way. Why? Because He loves you. Persistent faith brings you nearer to Him.

Father, help me to face every trial remembering that You are with me, teaching me, and drawing me nearer to You.

MEMORY VERSE OF THE DAY

I have no regrets. I couldn't be more sure of my ground—
the One I've trusted in can take care of what he's trusted me to do.

2 TIMOTHY 1:11–12 MSG

Morning

LORD, TAKE MY HAND.

God will hold your hand whenever you need Him. He isn't as impressed with what you do in life but with *how* you tackle each day. He wants you to know that He's there to take care of you, pick you up when you fall, and hold you in His loving arms.

God, teach me Your love. Let me feel Your embrace. I choose to trust in You.

Evening

HE IS ALWAYS AVAILABLE.

Are you sure that your heavenly Father is with you? When coming to grips with difficulties, do you turn to the Creator of the universe and ask for His help? You should. God is always available. He's always there. Just reach out and ask Him to take your hand. He will.

I believe, Father, with all my heart that You are with me.
Here is my hand. Take it and lead me.

MEMORY VERSE OF THE DAY

Create in me a clean heart, O God;
and renew a right spirit within me.

PSALM 51:10 KJV

Morning

TIME FOR A MAKEOVER?

Are you feeling sluggish and rundown this morning? Has your daily routine become a chore? God can fix that! He has the power to renew your heart and spirit. All you have to do is ask Him. He'll give you a supreme spiritual makeover, leaving you feeling refreshed, replenished, and rejuvenated.

Oh, God, I need a makeover. Renew my spirit.
Refresh me. Replenish my energy and enthusiasm.

Evening

I'M BEAUTIFUL, INSIDE AND OUT.

A new hairdo, makeup, a manicure, pedicure, and a new outfit—these make you lovely on the outside. But what about inside? Are you beautiful there, too? God wants you to be lovely inside and out. Confess your sins to Him tonight. Ask Him to give you a clean, godly heart.

Lord, forgive me for my sinfulness.
Thank You for making me beautiful—inside and out.

MEMORY VERSE OF THE DAY

The Lord my God will help you do everything needed.

1 Chronicles 28:20 cev

Morning

A LITTLE HELP, PLEASE.

What's on your to-do list today? At times, the list of tasks before you may seem overwhelming. You wonder how you'll ever get them all done. Relax. Take heart. God will give you the strength to do whatever needs to be done today. The rest can wait till tomorrow.

I put my day in Your hands, Lord. Guide me in prioritizing my tasks.

Evening

HE IS FIRST ON MY LIST.

Lists seem to grow all on their own! Too often you leave something off. You forget something important. If you make God the first item on every list—make Him your first priority—you can't go wrong. He will keep you calm and focused as you accomplish each and every task.

Dear God, I will write Your name at the top of my lists and trust You to guide me.

MEMORY VERSE OF THE DAY

Surely he took up our pain and bore our suffering.
ISAIAH 53:4 NIV

Morning ──────────────────────────────

HOW CAN I HELP YOU?

Physical pain affects not only the body, but also the spirit. Whether physical pain results from accident, disease, or aging, people sometimes need help keeping their spirits strong. God, of course, is the Great Helper, but you can help, too. Look around you today. Is someone hurting? How can you help them?

Jesus, open my eyes to those who are in physical pain.
Help me to help them put their faith in You.

Evening ──────────────────────────────

GOD UNDERSTANDS MY PAIN.

Often, no one can comfort you when you feel defeated by pain—no one except your Creator. He understands the pain you feel in every area of your life. You can look to Him for relief from all kinds of suffering. Pray to Him tonight, and ask Him to relieve your pain.

Lord, You know the source of my hurting, and You alone hold the cure.
Please, Lord Jesus, ease my pain.

MEMORY VERSE OF THE DAY

God will generously provide all you need. Then you will always have everything you need and plenty left over to share with others.

2 CORINTHIANS 9:8 NLT

Morning

HERE, HAVE SOME OF MINE.

Evaluate your needs against your wants. Can you admit that because of God's great generosity you have more than you can use? Share from your abundance today. Bring joy to someone. You will see more clearly the folly of seeking security in material possessions, much of which you don't need anyway.

Father God, You have blessed me with so very much!
Today I will share it with others.

Evening

THERE IS POWER IN GIVING.

There is power in giving, enough to lift you out of your reliance on "stuff." You can find new pleasure in participating in God's blessings and by sharing be doubly blessed in ways you could not have anticipated. After receiving His blessings, you can be part of God's provision to somebody else.

Lord, please shower me with blessings to share.
Open my eyes to those most in need.

MEMORY VERSE OF THE DAY

I was formed long ages ago, at the very beginning,
when the world came to be.

PROVERBS 8:23 NIV

Morning

GOD IS ETERNAL.

Men and women come along, filling in a narrow blip of time, and state that all of creation "just simply evolved." Don't let them fool you. God is the Great Creator, He existed before anything else. He designs, plans, and implements all that you see and everything you can't comprehend—today, and forever.

Lord, keep me from taking Your magnificence for granted.
Let my heart overflow with gratitude for all You are.

Evening

GOD IS IN CHARGE.

Somehow humans have turned around history believing that they are in charge. But, humans are not in charge. God is! Look around and you will see Him everywhere. He is still commanding the dawn to happen and the earth to keep spinning and the stars to remain in the sky. Aren't you glad?

Often, I forget to thank You for being so magnificently in control of the universe.
Thank You, Father, just for being YOU!

MEMORY VERSE OF THE DAY

*For it is God who is at work in you,
both to will and to work for His good pleasure.*

PHILIPPIANS 2:13 NASB

Morning —————————————————

I CAN BRING GOD PLEASURE.

God finds pleasure working inside of you. Every time you feed the poor, care for the sick, take care of your family, worship at His footstool, spend time with a loved one who's in pain—God is delighted. How wonderful to know that we can bring our Father such pleasure!

*Dear Heavenly Father,
I pray that everything I do today will be pleasing to Your sight.*

Evening —————————————————

GOD BRINGS ME DELIGHT.

The Bible tells us to delight ourselves in the Lord—to find fulfillment in Him. Too often when we dwell on worldly issues, we are blind to His eternal goodness. Tonight, think about all the ways that your heavenly Father brings enjoyment and fulfillment into your life. Then take time to praise Him.

*Dear God, You are so wonderful!
Your goodness surrounds me, and I am so blessed.*

MEMORY VERSE OF THE DAY

*And the LORD shall help them and deliver them; He shall deliver them
from the wicked, and save them, because they trust in Him.*

PSALM 37:40 NKJV

Morning

SPECIAL DELIVERY!

The Lord isn't just about delivering you from sin. He also longs to deliver you from selfishness, pain, and many other things that hold you back. He's in the "delivery" business! So what's required from you? Trust. When you place your trust in the Lord, you set yourself up for freedom.

*I trust You, O Lord.
Free me from sin and everything else that holds me back.*

Evening

I AM BORN AGAIN.

Think about that word "delivery." One of its definitions is "the process of giving birth." When God delivers you from sin and everything else, it is like being born again. If you haven't already done so, ask Jesus to come into your life and give you new birth. Trust Him as your Savior.

*Jesus, forgive me for my sins. I believe that You died for my sins
so I can have eternal life in heaven. Come into my heart and live there forever.*

MEMORY VERSE OF THE DAY

I can do all things through Him who strengthens me.
PHILIPPIANS 4:13 NASB

Morning

MISSION POSSIBLE!

It's a brand new day. Step into it with the attitude that there is nothing—absolutely nothing—you cannot do! There is no "mission impossible" when you are working through Christ. Your potential is limitless, and the possibilities are endless. Christ has already given you the boundless power and strength to succeed.

With You, Lord, I can do anything. Let's go!

Evening

DEAR LORD, I WANT TO. . .

Spend time tonight giving serious thought to a specific goal that you want to meet. Share that goal with your heavenly Father. With Philippians 4:13 written on your heart, acknowledge God's limitless power and strength working in you. Ask Him to guide you. Then trust Him to help you succeed.

Father, unleash Your power within me.
Guide me toward my goal as I put my trust in You.

MEMORY VERSE OF THE DAY

The LORD himself watches over you!
The LORD stands beside you as your protective shade.

PSALM 121:5 NLT

Morning

GOD IS MY SBF!

On days when the sun's rays are lethal, you need to be careful not to get burned. Like sunscreen on a hot, summer day, God is your SBF (Super Beneficent Father). Everyday, He is your ultimate protection. With Him always beside you, you'll have it made in the shade. How cool is that?

Thank You for protecting me, Father, no matter where I am.

Evening

I REST IN THE SHELTER OF HIS WINGS.

The Bible holds beautiful images of God's protection over us. Today's verse offers the image of Him providing shade from the sun's hot rays. Another verse, Psalm 61:4 NIV, refers to us taking refuge in the shelter of His wings. What other images can you think of that remind you of God's protecting love?

Lord, You are my help, and I rest tonight in the shelter of Your wings.

MEMORY VERSE OF THE DAY

You created my inmost being;
you knit me together in my mother's womb.

PSALM 139:13 NIV

Morning

I LOVE WHO I AM.

When you accepted Jesus as your Savior, you became a whole new person. He is on your side and always will be. He knows everything there is to know about you, and He has deemed you worthy of His love. Rejoice in the truth about who you are in Christ. Embrace the way God made you.

Jesus, I love who I am because God made me and You made me whole.

Evening

GOD LOVES ME.

No one knows you like God does. He created you to be who you are; He watched over you and protected you even before you were born. He welcomed you into His family, and He will love you throughout eternity. Nothing can ever change the fact that you are His and He loves you.

Thank You, God, for creating me,
knowing everything about me, and loving me just as I am.

MEMORY VERSE OF THE DAY

They sow the wind and they reap the whirlwind.

HOSEA 8:7 NASB

Morning

LIFT UP MY FAITH, LORD.

Wind can be gale-force strong or soft as a puff of air; devastating or beneficial. Whether a gentle breeze or a whirlwind, it is under God's authority. Today's verse illustrates the destruction that comes from disobedience. Be careful not to put your faith in worldly things. Remember who controls the wind.

Lift my faith, Lord, lift it as if on eagle's wings,
soaring high above worldly things.

Evening

GOD IS MY ONLY IDOL.

The world pulls us toward idolizing entertainers, sports figures, politicians, and others. They aren't gods, but imperfect human beings, just like you. If the winds of the world blow you toward idolatry, turn away. If you sow obedience to the Lord, you will reap calming breezes instead of destructive whirlwinds.

Dear God, I will make You my only God.
There is no one that comes near to Your greatness.

MEMORY VERSE OF THE DAY

Whatsoever ye do, do it heartily, as to the Lord, and not unto men.
C>COLOSSIANS 3:23 KJV

Morning

GOD IS THE BOSS OF ME!

It's easy to forget who your real boss is, especially in a demanding environment. No matter where you work, God wants you to do your work wholeheartedly, even when no one is looking. By pleasing the God in all you say and do, others will see Him through your work ethic.

God, keep reminding me that You are my boss.
My goal at work is to please You.

Evening

GOD KNOWS I AM QUALIFIED.

The person who supervises you and pays your wages deserves your best work, respect, and honesty—but you should remember that God is the one who blesses your employer. When you're promoted or receive a raise, you should give thanks to your Heavenly Father who is the best judge of your qualifications.

Father, please bless my employer.
Open his (or her) eyes to my work and my worthiness.

MEMORY VERSE OF THE DAY

*And even though you do not see [Jesus] now, you believe in him
and are filled with an inexpressible and glorious joy.*

1 Peter 1:8 niv

Morning

THERE IS JOY IN SALVATION.

Joy comes as a result of whom you trust, not in what you have. Joy is Jesus. When you find Jesus, "all things become new" as the Bible promises, and once again, you view the world through a child's eyes. Excitedly, you experience the "inexpressible and glorious joy" that salvation brings.

*Father, thank You for sending Jesus to save me.
Thank You for the joy that comes with salvation.*

Evening

THERE IS JOY IN THE LORD.

Joy isn't based on your circumstances. Its roots begin with the seed of God's Word planted in your heart. When you read and study His Word, your heart spills over with joy, knowing that the Lord loves and forgives you and that He is in complete control of your life.

*Dear God, thank You for loving me, forgiving me,
and taking control of my life. I love You!*

MEMORY VERSE OF THE DAY

I call on you, my God, for you will answer me;
turn your ear to me and hear my prayer.

PSALM 17:6 NIV

Morning

GOD IS ALWAYS AVAILABLE.

God can be reached at any hour of the day or night and every day of the year—including weekends and holidays! When you pray, you don't have to worry about disconnections, hang-ups, or poor reception. You will never be put on hold or your prayers diverted to another department. God is always available.

How wonderful it is, Lord, to know that You are always accessible to me,
for whatever I need, twenty–four hours a day.

Evening

HE HEARS ME.

God is eager to hear your petitions. He welcomes your prayers. The psalmist David wrote of God's response to those who put their trust in Him: "He will call upon me, and I will answer him" (Psalm 91:15 NIV). David had great confidence that God would hear his prayers. And you can, too!

I feel calm, heavenly Father, knowing that not only do You hear my prayers,
but You welcome them, too.

DAY 90

MEMORY VERSE OF THE DAY

"But he who enters by the door is a shepherd of the sheep.
To him the doorkeeper opens, and the sheep hear his voice,
and he calls his own sheep by name and leads them out."

JOHN 10:2–3 NASB

Morning

HE KNOWS MY NAME.

God knows your name. He knows and calls you by name, just as a shepherd knows and calls each of his sheep. God's relationship with you is unique as He leads you through life. Someday, when the Good Shepherd calls you home to heaven, you'll hear Him speak your name. Won't that be wonderful?

Good Shepherd, among all the people in the world, You know me by name.
Our relationship is loving and unique. How amazing!

Evening

I KNOW MY SHEPHERD'S VOICE.

These days, we hear some defend their heinous acts by saying, "The voices made me do it." Certainly the one they chose to listen to was not the voice of Jesus Christ. He is one hundred percent pure and good. He cannot contradict Himself. True sheep listen only for the voice of their Shepherd.

Lord, guide me to safe pastures today. Never leave me.

MEMORY VERSE OF THE DAY

Since we live by the Spirit, let us keep in step with the Spirit.

GALATIANS 5:25 NIV

Morning

HELP! I'M STUCK!

Picture yourself stuck in quicksand, unable to move forward or backward. Not a very pleasant feeling, is it? There's good news today! God's Word promises that you have the capability of reaching forward to what lies ahead. Focus on the Spirit, and allow Him to pull you out of the sand!

*Father, I feel stuck! Please,
help me to get out of this place and start moving forward.*

Evening

I'LL PUT THE PAST BEHIND ME.

If your feet are in quicksand, don't focus on your feet. Look up. Look ahead. Strain forward, even if it requires extreme levels of courage and strength. Put the past behind you once and for all. God is calling you to newer, bigger things, far beyond anything you anticipated.

*Dear God, I want to leave the past where it belongs—
in the past! Lead me forward. Let's go!*

MEMORY VERSE OF THE DAY

He put a new song in my mouth, a song of praise to our God.
Many people will see this and worship him.
Then they will trust the Lord.

Psalm 40:3 NCV

 Morning

I WILL PRAISE HIM WITH SINGING.

Do you love to sing? God promises to put a song in your mouth, and not just any song—He wants this joyous chorus to bubble up inside of you so that many will hear it and trust God, just like you do. Start warming up that voice right now!

Lord, I will praise You with singing.

Evening

MAKE A JOYFUL NOISE!

Maybe you say, "I'm not a good singer! I can't let anyone hear this voice of mine." (Maybe you're even cringing as you read this!) The Bible doesn't say we have to be good singers to praise the Lord; it simply says that we should "make a joyful noise" to Him. Anyone is capable of obedience.

Father God, no matter how bad I think I sound,
I know my song will be sweet music to Your ears.

MEMORY VERSE OF THE DAY

*"People look at the outward appearance,
but the LORD looks at the heart."*

1 SAMUEL 16:7 NIV

Morning

GOD THINKS THE WORLD OF ME!

Do you struggle against issues such as insecurity, body image, desire for love, and other worldly things? The standard for measure is usually the world's standards. Think about it: How can you be concerned about what the world thinks when the Creator of the universe thinks the world of you?

*Heavenly Father, that You think the world of me is all that matters.
Thank You! I love You.*

Evening

OH, TO BE LIKE JESUS.

You can free yourself from the impossible standard the world creates by looking to the truth of God's plan for you. That means accepting yourself as He made you. Your longing is satisfied in His perfect design for your individual destiny. Jesus is your standard, and in Him you always measure up.

*Jesus, thank You, for setting an example for me to follow,
and thank You for loving me just as I am.*

MEMORY VERSE OF THE DAY

The tongue has the power of life and death.

PROVERBS 18:21 NIV

Morning ———————————————————————

SAY WHAT?

Today, think about your words. Words can bring you down to the depths of despair. Despite what you know about God's grace, you can destroy your confidence and joy by participating in negative talk. It grieves the heart of God to hear His children slip under the weight of harmful words.

Dear Lord, remind me to be mindful of my words today.
Let my speech be pleasing to You.

Evening ———————————————————————

LORD, GUARD MY TONGUE.

Speaking the truth about God's love, forgiveness, favor, and mercy can give new life to your spirit and new inspiration to your soul. When you ask God to guard your tongue, you can be assured that He will give you uplifting words to speak to yourself and those around you.

Guard my tongue, Father. Help me to remember that
there is power in positive, uplifting words.

MEMORY VERSE OF THE DAY

"Arise! For this matter is your responsibility,
but we will be with you; be courageous and act."

Ezra 10:4 NASB

Morning

RAH! RAH! RAH!

Facing unexpected responsibility might fray your nerves. Fortunately, you can find the courage to act when others cheer you on and promise you support. Remember this: God is the leader of your cheering section. Seek friends and family to cheer you on. Be brave. Do what needs to be done!

Lord, I will rise and act in Your strength!

Evening

WITH A LITTLE HELP FROM MY FRIENDS.

Are you reluctant to ask for support? Don't be. Even Jesus, as He waited to be led away and crucified, asked His disciples to stay with Him and keep watch. When facing unexpected responsibility, when the task seems too hard, ask for a little help from your friends. It's perfectly alright to do so!

Heavenly Father, thank You for supportive friends.
Allow me to welcome them as trusted helpers.

MEMORY VERSE OF THE DAY

*May [God] give you the power to accomplish all the good
things your faith prompts you to do.*

2 Thessalonians 1:11 NLT

Morning

POWER UP!

It's time to power up for the day. God has already equipped you with the power to accomplish whatever your faith is calling you to do. What an awesome boost to your self-assurance! Start the day with this verse, and you will have confidence in everything. Walk tall, walk strong!

Lord, I walk confident that Your power is surging through me.

Evening

GOD'S WORD IS MINE!

Personalize today's verse. Make it your own. Say: "God is giving *me* the power to accomplish all the good things *my* faith prompts me to do." Make this your earnest and continuous prayer. Try doing this with other verses you have memorized from this book, and watch God work wonders in your life.

God, thank You for giving me power today to complete the tasks You called me to do.

MEMORY VERSE OF THE DAY

When you become successful, don't say, "I'm rich, and I've earned it all myself." Instead, remember that the LORD your God gives you the strength to make a living.

DEUTERONOMY 8:17–18 CEV

Morning

I'M RICH! NOW WHAT?

Riches don't impress God. He created everything we have, and it all belongs to Him. He can give a vast fortune and snatch it away just as easily. Instead of reveling in financial success, we should remember what an honor it is to serve as ambassadors for God's kingdom.

*Father, never allow me to become self–satisfied from success.
I know that all I have comes from You.*

Evening

GOD'S LOVE IS MY TREASURE.

God's abiding love is your treasure. And it's a treasure you can depend on—true riches that will never fail you. As God's ambassador, you have the protection of His diplomatic immunity, if not in this mortal life, then in the kingdom to come. You can rest comfortably in His assurance and hope.

*My Creator and Provider, thank You for blessing me
with Your unfailing love and assurance.*

MEMORY VERSE OF THE DAY

Since we have so great a cloud of witnesses surrounding us, let us also lay aside every encumbrance and the sin which so easily entangles us.

HEBREWS 12:1 NASB

Morning

FIND WHAT'S HIDDEN.

It's easy to recognize your obvious sins and undesirable thoughts. But what about the less obvious, sometimes even cherished, thoughts and habits that you hang on to? The Bible instructs you to discard anything that hinders your faith. Your heavenly Father supplies the courage and strength you need to do just that.

Lord, open my eyes today to anything hidden that gets in the way of my faith.

Evening

THROW OUT THE TRASH!

Do you spend too much time playing? Excess television watching, texting, surfing the web, and so many other diversions—all of it pulls you away from listening to God and doing His work. Tonight ask Him to forgive you and help you to get rid of anything that gets between you and Him.

*Dear God, forgive me for allowing trash to enter my life.
I don't want it! Help me to get rid of it for good.*

MEMORY VERSE OF THE DAY

And my God shall supply all your need
according to His riches in glory by Christ Jesus.

PHILIPPIANS 4:19 NKJV

Morning

GOD'S GOT IT COVERED.

God promises to meet your needs. That means you don't have to fret over where the next meal or clothing is coming from. He's got it covered—in His time and His own unique way. So, no worries. God, who owns the cattle on a thousand hills, can certainly meet your needs.

Father God, thank You for supplying all of my needs, each and every day.

Evening

EVERYTHING IS FROM HIM.

God is the One providing your every need. How about your job? God arranged it. The lower price on your new car? He was behind that, too. Your paycheck? Sure, it comes with your employer's name on it, but your real source is the Lord. Give that some thought tonight.

Thank You for everything, Lord, especially those things that I don't even notice!

MEMORY VERSE OF THE DAY

*Even though I walk through the darkest valley, I will fear no evil,
for you are with me; your rod and your staff, they comfort me.*

PSALM 23:4 NIV

Morning

GOD IS HERE!

When God shows up in a situation, fear disappears in an instant. Does that mean the "situation" instantly disappears? No, it doesn't. But knowing that the Lord is there with His arms around you will help so much. The journey through life's valleys is bearable when you're not alone.

*Put Your arms around me, Lord. Hold me up.
Let's walk through this valley together.*

Evening

SHELTER ME, LORD.

Here's a promise from God's Word: When you're really afraid, He promises to bring comfort. The valleys might be deep and the terrain unfamiliar, but God has a way of shining His light into even the deepest of places. Cry out to Him. Expect Him to pour His love and comfort over you.

*Father, I am so afraid! Shelter me under Your wings.
Comfort me with Your love.*

MEMORY VERSE OF THE DAY

"For the mountains may depart and the hills be removed, but my steadfast love shall not depart from you, and my covenant of peace shall not be removed," says the LORD, who has compassion on you.

ISAIAH 54:10 ESV

Morning

GOD'S LOVE IS STEADFAST.

Mountains are steadfast and immovable. Even small parts are not easily budged. Nature's forces take centuries or tremendous energy to do so. God says His love is even more immovable. Mountains will move before His love will leave you. Hills will depart easier than God would remove His covenant of peace with you.

Father, thank You for Your immovable love, for the permanence of Your covenant of peace.

Evening

GOD LOVES ME THROUGH JESUS.

Romans 5:1 (ESV) says, "Therefore, since we have been justified by faith, we have peace with God through our Lord Jesus Christ." Regardless of what you have done or will do, God's love is set upon you. By faith, you have only to believe what Jesus has done for you.

Jesus, thank You for saving me from sin. I have peace, knowing that I have eternal life in heaven.

MEMORY VERSE OF THE DAY

*Don't be concerned about the outward beauty of fancy hairstyles,
expensive jewelry, or beautiful clothes. You should clothe yourselves
instead with the beauty that comes from within, the unfading beauty
of a gentle and quiet spirit, which is so precious to God.*

1 Peter 3:3–4 NLT

Morning

WHAT SHALL I WEAR?

While fashion trends are fun, you can't forget where true beauty comes from.
It was Jesus who taught us not to place our treasure in physical things like our
bodies or worry about where we get our clothes. Jesus will transform your spirit
from rags to riches because He loves you.

Dear Jesus, I feel beautiful because You love me!

Evening

DESIGNER GOD.

Think about it: Shoes scuff, necklaces break, makeup wears off, and fabrics fade,
but true beauty starts from within. When you allow your heavenly Father to dress
your spirit in robes of love, joy, peace, patience, kindness, goodness, faithfulness,
gentleness, and self-control, your inner beauty will far outshine anything you wear.

*Father, I want to be a woman whose inner beauty shines,
so when people see me they see You and rejoice in Your creation.*

MEMORY VERSE OF THE DAY

If anyone is in Christ, he is a new creation;
old things have passed away; behold, all things have become new.

2 CORINTHIANS 5:17 NKJV

Morning

HE MAKES ALL THINGS NEW.

To "become" new implies an ongoing action. We are new in Jesus every day of our life. The old unproductive things drop away, leaving us with our regenerating life with Christ. When we grab hold of this truth, our eyes are opened to see what new things He has for us each day.

Open my eyes, Jesus! What do You have for me on this brand—new day?

Evening

RENEW MY FAITH, PLEASE.

Sometimes you might feel like you will never have that sense of newness that once characterized your life with God. What happened to the freshness of your faith, the sense of wonder that made you feel alive? Tonight, ask God to breathe new life into your faith. Then trust Him to do it.

Dear God, breathe new life into our relationship. Draw me nearer to You.

MEMORY VERSE OF THE DAY

"In this world you will have trouble. But take heart!
I have overcome the world."

JOHN 16:33 NIV

Morning ——————————————————

HE MAKES ALL THINGS NEW.

Troubling events in the world might rob you of your sense of security and well being. The rapid decline of morality, integrity, and godliness might make you question God and wonder why He doesn't fix everything. You need to remember that God is your fortress—and He has already won the battle.

Thank You, Lord, for reminding me that You have a battle plan,
and You will win the war.

Evening ——————————————————

JESUS IS MY REFUGE.

Jesus has already conquered sin—all the things that cause trouble. He wants you to remember that your home is not here on earth; it's in heaven. While you wait to join Him there, He is your sure and solid refuge from the devastating consequences of living in a sinful world.

Give me respite from troubling news, Jesus.
Wrap me in Your blanket of love.

MEMORY VERSE OF THE DAY

*"Well done, good and faithful servant! You have been faithful
with a few things; I will put you in charge of many things.
Come and share your master's happiness!"*

MATTHEW 25:21 NIV

Morning

IT'S A WIN–WIN SITUATION.

Make a list of things you do well, and ask God which ones He wants you to use in service to Him. When you use your talents, God rewards you for your efforts, invites you to share in His joy, and gives you a promotion to boot! It's a win-win situation.

I am Your servant, Lord. Show me what You want me to do.

Evening

HE TRUSTS ME, AND I TRUST HIM.

God has put His trust in you to be responsible with whatever tasks He has given you. As His trust in you builds, he will reward you with bigger and better responsibilities. Accept them joyfully. Remember this: Trust works both ways. Trust your Father to help with the big stuff.

*Thank You for trusting me, God. Now, help me to remember that
I don't have to do this alone.*

MEMORY VERSE OF THE DAY

I praise the LORD because he advises me.
Even at night, I feel his leading.

PSALM 16:7 NCV

Morning

TODAY WILL BE AWESOME!

Get ready for an awesome day! You know it will be great because God is your advisor. Throughout the day, if only you listen to His whisperings, He will impart wisdom and lead you forward in great and amazing ways. Now, get out there and have a God-filled, awesome day!

O, Lord, I praise You! Thank You for leading me with Your wisdom.

Evening

I CAN'T SLEEP.

All of that awesomeness might have left you with your brain still racing. There's no need to lay awake, thinking. God provides guidance anytime day and night. Ask Him to help you go to sleep. Give Him those racing thoughts. Close your eyes. Whisper His name. "Good night, Dear God. Good night."

Father, shut off my thoughts. Bless me with sweet sleep as I rest in Your love.

MEMORY VERSE OF THE DAY

*[Jesus said,] "I came so they can have real and eternal life,
more and better life than they ever dreamed of."*

JOHN 10:10 MSG

Morning

SMILE!

You have been blessed with an abundant life. That should put a smile on your face. So, show the world! Make it a point today to smile at everyone you meet. Say a friendly, "Hello." Allow God's light to radiate through you. You'll be surprised by those who smile back.

O, Lord, I praise You! Thank You for leading me with Your wisdom.

Evening

I WILL LIVE LIFE ABUNDANTLY.

How would you evaluate your life? Good? Bad? Ugly? Christ came to give you—yes, you!—an *abundant* life. That includes salvation, healing, sustenance, and more. Trust Him, and your life can be more beautiful than you can ever dream or imagine—for eternity! You can't ask for anything better than that.

*Father, forgive me for letting life get me down.
Fill me up with life's beauty, abundantly, spilling over!*

MEMORY VERSE OF THE DAY

*"Come to me, all you who are weary and burdened,
and I will give you rest."*

MATTHEW 11:28 NIV

Morning

I NEED A BREAK!

Are you overdue for a break? If so, ask the Lord to show you how you can take Him up on this promise: that you can come to Him (weary and heavy-laden) and experience true rest and refreshment. He will do it! You simply have to take the time to meet Him there. Ah, rest!

*Dear Father God, I'm worn out. I need a break.
Here I am, Lord. Grant me rest.*

Evening

TAKE A DAY OFF.

You zip, zip, zip from one thing to another, barely pausing to breathe. God never intended for you to be on the go 'round the clock. In fact, His Word is pretty clear that we're meant to take a sabbatical once a week—Sunday! Schedule a day of rest today. You deserve it.

Father, I need to slow down. Thank You for wanting me to rest. I'll do it!

MEMORY VERSE OF THE DAY

But as many as received Him, to them He gave the right to become children of God, to those who believe in His name.

JOHN 1:12 NKJV

Morning

BUT, I'M A GROWNUP!

You might be a grownup, but to God, you are one of His kids. Imagine how He must feel when he gazes into your face. What joy it must bring your heavenly Father to dote on you, to care for your every need, and to provide you with infinite blessings.

I sometimes forget, God, that You see me as a child still in need of Your guidance. Thank You for being my loving Father.

Evening

I WILL MAKE HIM PROUD.

We have a right to be children of God because we believe in His Name. With that right comes a responsibility—to make our heavenly Father proud. What have you done today to please Him? God loves you just as you are, but He feels pure joy when you make Him proud.

Father, whatever I do, I will strive to please You. Why? Because I love You!

MEMORY VERSE OF THE DAY

*And these things happened as examples for us,
to stop us from wanting evil things as those people did.*

1 Corinthians 10:6 NCV

Morning

I CAN LEARN FROM GOD'S PEOPLE.

By reading the Bible, you will learn from God's dealings with people throughout history to not fall into the same traps. Twenty-three thousand died in one day because they worshipped pagan gods, refusing to obey the one true God. As you read about people and their struggles in God's Word, learn from them.

*I am discovering, God, that the Bible is full of examples
that apply to my own life. Thank You for them.*

Evening

I'LL STAY AWAY FROM SIN.

How can you stop yourself from falling into sin? By trying not to give in to the same temptations that people have faced throughout history. No one is perfect. God knows that. But when you willfully keep sinning, like some of the people in the Bible did, you please Satan, not God.

Father, help me to avoid temptation by taking one step closer to You.

MEMORY VERSE OF THE DAY

There is no distinction between Greek and Jew,
circumcised and uncircumcised, barbarian, Scythian,
slave and freeman, but Christ is all, and in all.

COLOSSIANS 3:11 NASB

Morning

LET'S ALL GET ALONG.

Is there prejudice in your heart? To say you love Jesus and yet maintain deeply rooted prejudices against others is inconsistent with everything He taught. Jesus came to reconcile all people to Himself, not separate them into factions. We all belong to God. Remember that today. Open your heart to others.

Dear Lord, if there is any prejudice in my heart,
make me aware, and wash it away.

Evening

I WILL BE A PEACEMAKER.

The Bible has many stories about people not getting along. Watch for them as you read. Ask yourself what might have brought peace. God sent Jesus to bring us into reconciliation with Him. When you read about Jesus, you will see that He was a peacemaker in all situations. You should be, too.

Jesus, I want to bring peace and reconciliation into difficult circumstances.
Guide me, please.

MEMORY VERSE OF THE DAY

"This is its meaning: The seed is God's message to men."
LUKE 8:11 TLB

Morning

GOD'S WORD IS IN MY HEART.

Each scripture verse you memorize is like a seed God plants in your heart.
Whether or not it grows depends on you. Are you thinking about the verses as
you memorize them? Are you applying them to your life? If so, then the seed God
planted is growing—and so is your faith!

Father, I will learn and meditate on the scriptures You give me.
I will apply them to my life.

Evening

HEAR YE, HEAR YE!

In this age of instant information, we forget that town criers once walked streets
shouting important news. The story of Jesus is called "The Good News." It is
meant to be shared. Think of yourself as God's town crier. Share what you know
about Jesus. Don't be shy! Shout it to the world!

Jesus, Your story is too wonderful not to be shared.
I will tell others about You, without apprehension.

MEMORY VERSE OF THE DAY

You are complete in Him, who is the head of all principality and power.
COLOSSIANS 2:10 NKJV

Morning

JESUS COMPLETES ME.

Imagine what life would be like if you had no awareness of Jesus' power and desire to provide everything that you need to reflect His glory. His offer of the opportunity to be complete in Him is a genuine demonstration of what He is prepared to share with you—which is everything!

Jesus, like that movie saying goes: "You complete me!"
Thank You for being my everything.

Evening

JESUS' POWER IS MINE.

Jesus' authority over evil becomes part of you. You can access His power. Believing in Him leads into a privileged relationship with God that leaves you wanting nothing. You can tap into the authority He has given you. You don't have to settle for less; you have it all—all that Jesus is!

Remind me always, Jesus, that Your power flows through me.
It is mine, whenever I need it.

MEMORY VERSE OF THE DAY

But Jesus often withdrew to lonely places and prayed.

LUKE 5:16 NIV

Morning

SOLITUDE IS GOOD.

You are God's hands and feet in this world, and He can use you in mighty ways. But He also calls you to rest and pray. Jesus put a priority on this, frequently leaving the crowd to seek solitude. He encourages you to do the same. Make quiet prayer your priority today.

Father, allow me to say no to something today so that I might say yes to quiet time with You.

Evening

JUST YOU AND ME, GOD.

Were all sorts of demands put on you today? Did you feel pulled at from every angle? This evening, slow down and have some alone time with God. Find a place that is quiet where you can pray. Jesus modeled this for you. He wants you to find rest in Him.

Show me the importance of rest, Dear God. Teach me to rest in You.

MEMORY VERSE OF THE DAY

"For I, the LORD your God, hold your right hand; it is I who say to you, 'Fear not, I am the one who helps you.'"

ISAIAH 41:13 ESV

Morning

MY HAND IN GOD'S.

God holds your hand. He protects you and comforts you. He is with you in your most anxious moments and in your darkest hours. With the clasp of His hand comes courage for any situation. He tells you not to be afraid. Why? Because He has a hold of you.

Almighty God, I am grateful that You hold my hand. Forgive me for the times I have forgotten this and allowed fear to reign my life.

Evening ———

YOUR HAND IN MINE.

In times of great emotion, you grab the hand of a nearby friend or family member; it says, "I am with you." You clasp the hand of a sick loved one; your hand tells them you are present, suffering with them. With every gripping of another's hand, you are extending the hand of God.

My Comforter and Protector, lead me to those in need; extend Your hand to them through mine.

MEMORY VERSE OF THE DAY

"I am the Lord, and I do not change."
Malachi 3:6 nlt

Morning

GOD DOES NOT CHANGE.

In this world, change is the one thing you can count on. But God is not of this world. He is supernatural, otherworldly. And He does not change. His strength, saving grace, and power are a sure thing no matter where, no matter when. Count on it! Count on Him today.

What a relief, God, that I can always depend on You.

Evening

HE LIFTS ME UP!

People will often let you down. It's human nature. Whether intended or not, your friends and family members sometimes won't live up to your expectations. When that happens, remember—they are only human. You can always depend on God to lift you up when others let you down.

Father God, I can trust You to never let me down.
Now, help me to forgive those who do.

MEMORY VERSE OF THE DAY

*You keep him in perfect peace whose mind is stayed on you,
because he trusts in you.*

ISAIAH 26:3 ESV

Morning

HIS PEACE IS PERFECT.

When your eyes are on God, everything else fades to gray—problems seem smaller, enemies weaker, and sorrows dimmer. If your eyes are fixed only on Him, you will experience a peace beyond all understanding. Focus on God today. And if you find yourself slipping out of focus, ask Him to reset your sight.

All-Powerful God, help me to see clearly today by focusing my thoughts on You.

Evening

I CAN HAVE PERFECT PEACE.

Try this tonight, in bed, before you sleep. Meditate on today's verse. Then close your eyes and imagine yourself alone by a quiet stream. Listen to the water as it flows across the rocks. As you begin to fall asleep, feel God's spirit flowing over you and in you. Oh. . .what peace!

Heavenly Father, I will sleep in perfect peace trusting that You watch over me.

MEMORY VERSE OF THE DAY

*Put on the full armor of God, so that. . .you may be able to stand
your ground, and after you have done everything, to stand.*

EPHESIANS 6:13 NIV

Morning

GOD'S ARMOR PROTECTS ME.

The Bible says that God's armor is the belt of truth, the breastplate of righteousness, your feet fitted with readiness that comes from the gospel of peace, the shield of faith, and the helmet of salvation. Put on His armor before you leave the house today, and nothing—nothing!—can harm you.

*With all Your armor covering me, God,
I am ready for anything. Thank You!*

Evening

I WILL STAND.

Sometimes, all you can do is stand in God's armor while the enemy's arrows strike you. One after another, they try to break through to your flesh. But you know that they can't! God's armor is impenetrable. When the enemy fires, don't run; stand firm. God protects you. He won't let you fall.

*Almighty Father, when the battle rages and I can't fight back,
I will trust that Your armor protects me.*

MEMORY VERSE OF THE DAY

The righteous lead blameless lives;
blessed are their children after them.

PROVERBS 20:7 NIV

Morning

HOW CAN I BLESS MY CHILDREN?

Want to know the best possible way to bless your children? Live a righteous life. When you live a life pleasing to God, He is watching—and blessing. You are leaving a very special legacy for your children, and this makes Him happy. He, in turn, bestows blessing upon blessing.

God, help me to set the best example for my children by living
in a way that is pleasing to You.

Evening

WHAT IF I STRUGGLE WITH SIN?

If you're struggling with sin in your life, it's not just important to overcome it for your own sake, but the sake of your children. Let the "family blessing" begin with you. Righteous living will turn things around for the whole family. The legacy will be remarkable, and it can all start with you.

Father, help me to overcome the sin in my life,
for my sake and for my children.

MEMORY VERSE OF THE DAY

"For I will forgive their wickedness and will remember their sins no more."
HEBREWS 8:12 NIV

Morning ——————————————————

FORGIVE AND FORGET.

How can God—the all-knowing—not only forgive, but possibly forget our sins? He promises to do so. If only we could forget when we forgive others for the things they've done to wound us. What a blissful situation, to have no recollection of the past wrongs done to us.

God, help me not only to forgive those who have harmed me,
but also to put it out of my mind.

Evening ——————————————————

IT'S HIS CHOICE.

God chooses to forgive your sins. It's a deliberate effort on His part. And notice, today's scripture doesn't say "sin." The word is "sins" (plural). We're tempted on every front. There's much to overcome, but we have this proof that overcoming all sinful behavior really is possible. Praise the Lord!

Lord, I praise You for forgiving my sins—and for choosing to forget them!

MEMORY VERSE OF THE DAY

*"Until now you have not asked for anything in my name.
Ask and you will receive, and your joy will be complete."*

JOHN 16:24 NIV

Morning

I ASK IN JESUS' NAME.

Asking in Jesus' name puts you in line with His will for what your wants should be and what your needs really are. With a Christ-like mind, the more likely you are to want the best things, the right things. This is what brings the joy—knowing you are one with Christ in your desires.

God, for what I have asked of You, in Jesus' name I pray. Amen.

Evening

I HAVE CONFIDENCE IN JESUS.

You can be confident knowing you have just what you need when you have asked and received what God's will for you is. Confidence brings joy, and receiving what truly fulfills your longings brings you full circle. You are complete and satisfied when you ask and receive in gratitude, praising Jesus for your joy.

Jesus, thank You for knowing what I need and giving me what is right and best.

MEMORY VERSE OF THE DAY

My eyes are always on the LORD,
for he rescues me from the traps of my enemies.

PSALM 25:15 NLT

Morning

I WILL FOLLOW JESUS.

When your concentration strays from Jesus, you risk going your own way and falling into the enemy's traps. Jesus wants to show you the safe path, the one that goes around the enemy of your soul. He walks ahead of you, looking back to see if you are following Him—so, follow Him today!

Jesus, I pray that when You look behind You today,
You will see me following You.

Evening

JESUS LEADS MY WAY.

Jesus never leaves you behind. You can try to rush ahead of Him, but He is never behind you—He is always in front, removing the snares from your path. Thanks to Jesus, you don't have to walk blindly into danger. He is always there to safely guide you.

Thank You, Jesus, for gently holding me back when I try to race ahead of You.

MEMORY VERSE OF THE DAY

See then that ye walk circumspectly, not as fools, but as wise,
redeeming the time, because the days are evil.

EPHESIANS 5:15–16 KJV

Morning

I WILL TELL OTHERS ABOUT JESUS.

Tell someone about Jesus today. Your primary desire should be to help people know Him. This doesn't mean that all you ever do is talk about God, but when He gives you opportunities, you should take them. No matter what you do or say, your actions should always set a Christ-like example.

Dear God, open up opportunities today for me to share Jesus
with my coworkers and friends.

Evening

I WILL USE MY TIME WISELY.

Your time on earth is not everlasting, and you should use every minute wisely. In heaven, you will give an account of all your time, whether you wasted it or used it for God's glory. That's why it is so important to look often at how you measure up to God's expectations for you.

O God, give me a desire to make every moment I have count for You.
Help me be wise in how I conduct my life.

MEMORY VERSE OF THE DAY

"Hold tight to GOD, your God, just as you've done up to now."
JOSHUA 23:8 MSG

Morning ———————————————————————————

DON'T LET GO!

Sometimes, life might come at you so fast that you just want to give up. Hang on with faith. Don't let go! The enemy of your soul wants you to quit. You've gotten this far in your faith believing that God will keep His promises and help you reach your destiny. Don't stop now.

Father God, when I feel like quitting, take my hand and lead me.

Evening ———————————————————————————

HOLD ON TIGHT!

When you don't think you can take another step—hold tight to God's hand. Tomorrow will give you a fresh start with the strength you need to go a little further. Take a deep breath, get a fresh grasp on your faith, and hang on. God will help you to reach your goal.

Lord, help me to hold fast to You so I can make it through all the circumstances of life no matter how tough they seem.

MEMORY VERSE OF THE DAY

*"If you forgive others for their transgressions,
your heavenly Father will also forgive you."*

Matthew 6:14 nasb

Morning

HURT HAPPENS.

People may hurt you without meaning to. Often, their offense is hurtful to them, too. God wants you to show mercy to the person who caused the pain. A gentle response is a reflection of God's character. He provided you with the ability to forgive because He forgave *you*. Whom do you need to forgive today?

*Lord God, help me to forgive _____ today.
And thank You for forgiving me!*

Evening

I'M SORRY!

Were you at fault? Have you hurt someone? When the fault is yours, demonstrate humility, freely admitting your fault, taking responsibility. Ask for forgiveness. God has a way of working things out for good. The one you wronged might discover the Lord through you, when you apologize sincerely in a godly way.

*O, Father, help me to know when I am wrong,
and to take responsibility for my actions.*

MEMORY VERSE OF THE DAY

You are of God. . .He who is in you is greater than he who is in the world.

I JOHN 4:4 NKJV

Morning

CELEBRATE!

You have something to celebrate today, and every day: The Spirit of God lives within you, right now and always! Nothing in this world—people, problems, evils, losses, greed, grief, terror—is mightier than He! Plant that thought deep in your mind this morning, and your confidence, your spirit, will thrive!

Heavenly Father, today I will celebrate Your greatness.
Thank You for making Your home in my heart.

Evening

GOD IS THE GREATEST.

Isn't it awesome that God, the one-and-only, know all, do all God, dwells with you all the time inside your heart? When you think of the most powerful world leader ever, who comes first to your mind? It should be God! His power exceeds that of any world leader, past, present, or future.

Lord, You are awesome, mighty AND— the greatest Person in my life!

MEMORY VERSE OF THE DAY

"When you pass through the waters, I will be with you; and through the rivers, they shall not overflow you. When you walk through the fire, you shall not be burned, nor shall the flame scorch you."

ISAIAH 43:2 NKJV

Morning

THROUGH IT ALL. . .

God doesn't promise that you won't have problems. But He does promise to be with you when you do. He is by your side, keeping you afloat in the "flood." He'll keep you from getting burned in the "fire." He is the One who will never, ever leave you. That's true love!

Thank You, God, for always being by my side. I know I can count on You!

Evening

GOD IS WITH ME.

As you dig deeper into God's Word, and memorize scripture, be watchful for stories about God's heroes. There are many in the Bible: Moses, David, Paul, and others. Their dedication to God in the midst of their troubles will bolster your faith! Read their stories. Allow them to teach you.

Father God, lead me to the heroes in the Bible, and allow their stories to strengthen my faith.

MEMORY VERSE OF THE DAY

*Freely (without pay) you have received,
freely (without charge) give.*
MATTHEW 10:8 AMPC

Morning ――――――――――――――――――――――――――――

FREELY I HAVE RECEIVED.

God has given you so many gifts. He gives you love and affection to keep you moving in the righteous direction. Everything you are, everything you have, has been given to you by God, overflowing, and free. Share His gifts with others today, and trust that God will continue to provide.

Thank You, God, for Your precious gifts. Be with me, now, as I give to others.

Evening ――――――――――――――――――――――――――――

FREELY I WILL GIVE.

Make a plan to give something, secretly. The Bible warms about giving to others *only* so others will see your charity (Matthew 6:1). There are few things more satisfying than secretly giving to others. Bestow an anonymous gift on a friend, family member, or neighbor, and watch them revel in their unexpected blessing.

*Father, who needs a little blessing tomorrow?
What can I do in secret to brighten up their day?*

MEMORY VERSE OF THE DAY

*Yet he did not waver through unbelief regarding the promise of God,
but was strengthened in his faith and gave glory to God,
being fully persuaded that God had power
to do what he had promised.*

ROMANS 4:20–21 NIV

Morning

I'M GROWING!

Just like children grow and change, Christians also grow as believers. Your spiritual growth depends on spending time in God's Word and praying. How fun, to think that you're growing in your faith! How pleased God must be when He looks at the changes going on in your heart and life.

*Heavenly Father, every day I feel our relationship becoming stronger.
I love this growing, changing process!*

Evening

CHANGE IS GOOD.

Change is good, but as you grow and change, you have to remain steady in your belief—unmoved by the various changes you're going through. When you do this, you will be strengthened in your faith and more convinced than ever that God will do amazing things in and through you.

*Change isn't always easy, Father, and when it isn't,
please help me to remain steady in my faith.*

MEMORY VERSE OF THE DAY

*"Those who hate you will be clothed with shame,
and the dwelling place of the wicked will come to nothing."*

JOB 8:22 NKJV

 Morning

SHAME, SHAME, SHAME!

Those who love the Lord are "dressed" in His finest (joy, peace, strength, and so on). Today's verse says that those who oppose God's ways will be clothed in shame. They will wear shame like a cloak. So, if someone does you wrong, don't worry. God will put them to shame!

*God, I give to You all the insults and wrongdoings done to me by others.
Shame them, if You please.*

Evening

DON'T INSULT MY FATHER!

If someone slanders God, don't fret. The Lord has His own way of taking care of those who insult Him. Just keep wearing His clothing—mercy, grace, joy—and let Him deal with the wardrobe of others. Your Christ-like example might be just the poke they need to shape up and seek God.

*Father, if someone speaks of You in a negative way,
help me to respond as Jesus would.*

MEMORY VERSE OF THE DAY

"It is the LORD who goes before you."
DEUTERONOMY 31:8 ESV

Morning

THE LORD GOES BEFORE ME.

When you are heading into unknown territory, it's a relief to know that someone has gone ahead of you to secure your destination. A guide is of great value to someone unsure of what might lie ahead. The Lord is your guide. Ask Him to go before you today.

Lord, I don't know what lies ahead, but You do.
Guide me to it and through it.

Evening

HE PREPARES FOR ME.

Jesus is way ahead of you, taking care of every detail of your journey, preparing safe havens where you can rest in His protection, and building a dwelling place for you when you get there. He has it all under His control—and He always has your best interests at heart.

Jesus, You know where I am going, and You have prepared everything
for when I get there. Thank You!

MEMORY VERSE OF THE DAY

Because of his glory and excellence,
he has given us great and precious promises.

2 Peter 1:4 nlt

Morning ──────────────────────────

GOD KEEPS HIS WORD.

People may let you down, but God never will. His Word offers hundreds of promises, and He is more than able to deliver them. God's motivation is love, which is the very definition of who He is. God cannot fail, He will not disappoint, and He does what He says He will do.

Dear Father, I praise You because You never disappoint.
You never let me down.

Evening ──────────────────────────

PROMISES, PROMISES!

Think about the scripture verses you have memorized so far. Many of them are God's promises. The Bible is overflowing with His promises. All you have to do is claim them for yourself, and then trust God to fulfill them. People may let you down because of their humanity, but God never will.

Dear God, Your promises are precious, and they are all for me!
I claim them as my own.

MEMORY VERSE OF THE DAY

Jesus replied: "'Love the Lord your God with all your heart and with all your soul and with all your mind.' This is the first and greatest commandment. And the second is like it: 'Love your neighbor as yourself.'"
MATTHEW 22:37–39 NIV

Morning

I WALK THE "LOVE TALK."

When you say, "I love you," do you mean it? Telling someone you love them and showing love are two very different things. Let's face it—some people are harder to love than others. But God wants us to walk the love talk, always, not just when we want to, or when it's convenient.

Lord, I promise to love You and my neighbor with my whole heart.

Evening

HOW DO I LOVE THEE?

It may not always be convenient to love God, but His love for you is turned on 24/7. He never puts you on hold or doles out love in rationed amounts. He's never too busy or takes a day off from loving you. Can you say the same about how you love Him?

Heavenly Father, forgive me for not loving You enough.
Help me to love You more!

MEMORY VERSE OF THE DAY

*The LORD bless thee, and keep thee; the LORD make his face
shine upon thee, and be gracious unto thee.*

NUMBERS 6:24–25 KJV

 Morning

BLESS HIS HOLY NAME.

Once you have a relationship with God the Father through Jesus Christ, you are
in line for a multitude of blessings. God's love for you is eternal, as are His gifts.
So, open your arms and become a thankful recipient for all He's given. Praise Him
and bless His holy name.

*Lord, You have given me so much, and I am thankful.
Let me give thanks for Your gifts.*

Evening

ZERO IN ON HIS BLESSINGS.

Why is it difficult to recognize every blessing? Because it's human nature to zero
in on what's wrong and miss what's very right. You can overcome that habit by
praising and spending time with God. When you bless Him in faithful praise, He
will bless you. How has God blessed you today?

*Dear God, open my eyes to all the ways You bless me.
I am grateful, God! So grateful.*

MEMORY VERSE OF THE DAY

*The LORD their God will save his people on that day as a shepherd
saves his flock. They will sparkle in his land like jewels in a crown.*

ZECHARIAH 9:16 NIV

Morning

I AM A JEWEL. . .

When you accepted Christ you became a crown jewel! With divine precision, He
painstakingly chiseled away the ugly rough spots. He applied heat and pressure
for your clarity, and then polished you until you glistened. Jesus made you a
gemstone from crude rock to form a jewel worthy of a setting in His crown.

*Jesus, thank You for saving me. You accepted me just as I was
and made me into a crown jewel!*

Evening

. . .AND I WILL SPARKLE!

You are a jewel in progress. In your transformation, God asks you to wait patiently
as He does His work. In His perfect time, you will reflect the perfect firelight of His
brilliance. Until then, sparkle! Do all that you can to be a reflection of Him. Show
His fine work to the world.

*O, Lord, You are doing such good works within me.
Let Your goodness radiate from me! Let it shine!*

MEMORY VERSE OF THE DAY

If we walk in the Light as He Himself is in the Light, we have fellowship with one another, and the blood of Jesus His Son cleanses us from all sin.

1 JOHN 1:7 NASB

Morning

WHAT IF THE LIGHTS GO OUT?

Losing faith in God is like a power outage—nothing works and it's hard to see. But when you live in submission to His authority, He will light your way. With the Lord at your side, you have no reason to fear a power outage. . .today, and every day, God is your Light.

Almighty God, my day is in Your hands.
I trust You to be my Light and guide me.

Evening

SIN HIDES IN THE SHADOWS.

Like the undetected obstacle that stubs your toe in darkness, sin hides in the shadows wanting to make you fall. But God's Light is with you to avert that danger. Dark and light cannot occupy the same space. Even at dusk, a trace of light holds back the night, if only for a moment.

God, thank You! Thank You for holding back the darkness
and allowing me to see clearly.

MEMORY VERSE OF THE DAY

David was greatly distressed because the men were talking
*of stoning him. . . . But David found strength in the L*ORD *his God.*

1 SAMUEL 30:6 NIV

Morning

I WILL TRUST IN GOD.

Are you upset about what someone said? When hurtful, worrisome words echo in your ears, drown them out with a prayer to the God Almighty. He will give you strength and shield you from the slings and arrows of others. Like David, in today's memory verse, put your trust in Him.

Lord, fill my mind with Your good words and my heart with Your awesome strength.

Evening

GOD IS MY CHAMPION.

David believed it: God is bigger than anything and anybody. Imagine it. There is nothing that can stand up to Him! God is the great Conqueror. He wins every war. So, be fearless! Be brave! Be confident! With God as your champion, you will be triumphant in every battle.

Father, You are my strength and my confidence.
In every battle, I will put my faith in You.

MEMORY VERSE OF THE DAY

Wait for the LORD; be strong and let your heart take courage;
yes, wait for the LORD.

PSALM 27:14 NASB

 Morning ─────────────────────────

I WILL WAIT FOR HIM.

Courage is framed by patience in the Lord and trust that He will bring about what He has promised in your life. If you feel like running on ahead of Him, wait—and wait some more. If you dig into ensured expectation that His promises will be realized, then your courage will grow.

As I walk by faith, Lord, I become stronger every day.

Evening ─────────────────────────

I WILL SEEK HIM FIRST.

When you trust in God's willingness, readiness, and ability to provide you with what you need, you'll no longer be preoccupied with the essentials. Then you can put your focus on what God wants you to do. Endeavor to seek Him first, and all the rest will fall into place.

I come seeking You, God, knowing that You'll handle the rest.

MEMORY VERSE OF THE DAY

Anxiety weighs down the heart, but a kind word cheers it up.

PROVERBS 12:25 NIV

Morning

WORDS. . .WORDS. . .WORDS!

What kind of words are you speaking to yourself and others? Words of kindness or sharp, critical ones? Words can build up or tear down. God didn't put humans on earth to cut others down or to offer critique. His Holy Spirit does a far better job. Speak only kind words today!

Dear God, today I will watch my words and to use them to build others up.

Evening

ENCOURAGING WORDS.

Some people try to fix others with their words. Instead of trying to "fix" them, it is better to speak gentle words of encouragement. That way, their hearts will be more open to God's correction and direction. With your words, strive to lift spirits. Then let God do the rest.

Lord, if I slip into "fix mode," stop me!
Remind me to be an encourager, not a discourager.

MEMORY VERSE OF THE DAY

"The eternal God is your refuge, and underneath are the everlasting arms;
He will thrust out the enemy from before you, and will say, 'Destroy!' "
DEUTERONOMY 33:27 NKJV

Morning

GOD IS MY SAFE PLACE.

Imagine your ultimate dream home—your "safe" place to dwell. Then remember this: the very safest—and most luxurious—place to live is in God's presence. How do you get there? By spending time with Him. In that place, He provides comfort, security, joy, peace, and all of the other things you need.

Father God, You are my safe place.
I know that in Your presence, I have all that I need.

Evening

HE DEFENDS ME.

When you take refuge in God's presence, He serves as your defender. He pushes the enemy away and surrounds you with a vast army of angels, ready to protect you. Maybe you'll never get to dwell in the dream house of your imagination, but God's dwelling place is so much more!

Dear God, I love coming into Your presence where
I know everything is safe, all the time.

MEMORY VERSE OF THE DAY

*Having predestined us to adoption as sons by Jesus Christ to Himself,
according to the good pleasure of His will.*

EPHESIANS 1:5 NKJV

Morning

WHO AM I REALLY?

Have you ever wondered, *Who am I really*? Like an adopted child, you are chosen.
Even before the foundation of the world was set in place, God chose *you* to be
His child. He created you for His pleasure and brought you into His family for your
blessing. That's who you are—really!

*God when I question my identity,
remind me of what really matters—I am Yours!*

Evening

I AM CHOSEN.

Who wouldn't want to be chosen to have a relationship with the Creator
of the universe? To be chosen for such a purpose is far beyond our human
comprehension, and yet it is the truth about the Father's love and desire for you—
and about your identity.

*How wonderful it is to know that You chose me to be Yours!
You wanted me, You made me, and You love me!*

MEMORY VERSE OF THE DAY

He who is joined to the Lord is one spirit with Him.

1 Corinthians 6:17 nkjv

Morning ───────────────────────

OUR RELATIONSHIP IS ETERNAL.

Human relationships are fragile and too often broken by circumstances. Even the best earthly union is only valid until death. But our union with Christ is in the deepest sense an unbreakable, lasting covenant. The joy and strength you receive from joining your spirit with the living God lasts through eternity.

Almighty God, how wonderful it is to know that You and I are forever!

Evening ───────────────────────

I AM ONE WITH GOD.

You are one in the Spirit with the Creator. He loves you so much that He reaches down in grace to pull you to Him. You must never lose sight of the glorious truth that allowing you to become one with Him was His choice. He wants you to participate in His reality.

O, Lord, Your Spirit and mine are joined together—and because of that,
I will never be alone. Thank You!

MEMORY VERSE OF THE DAY

Why, my soul, are you downcast? Why so disturbed within me?
Put your hope in God, for I will yet praise him,
my Savior and my God.

PSALM 42:5 NIV

Morning

I HOPE. . .

When circumstances make you feel depressed, remember that you have hope. Hope that your circumstances will not always be the way they are right now. Hope that no matter how dismal your situation seems, God is in control, and He will win this battle for you. Allow yourself to hope today!

Father, when I am depressed, I will remember that You are in control of the situation—You are still God!

Evening

HOPE IS ALL AROUND ME.

Hope is like a little green shoot poking up through hard, cracked ground. When you're depressed, give that shoot some fertilizer and make it grow! Pour out your heart to God. And don't carry the burden alone. Seek help from a trusted friend or godly counselor. Look for hope. It's all around you.

Heavenly Father, help me to find a ray of hope in the midst of every dark situation.

DAY 144

MEMORY VERSE OF THE DAY

Because of the LORD's great love we are not consumed, for his compassions
never fail. They are new every morning; great is your faithfulness.

LAMENTATIONS 3:22–23 NIV

Morning

TODAY IS A NEW BEGINNING.

God starts out His day offering renewed compassion to His children. No matter
what trials, difficulties, and sins yesterday brought, the morning ushers in a fresh
experience, a brand-new beginning for believers who seek His forgiveness. All
you have to do is accept His gift. Today is a brand-new day!

God, Your promise of never—ending compassion for me is amazing!
I never want to take for granted the grace You offer every day.

Evening

TOMORROW I CAN TRY AGAIN.

Are you burdened from today's stress? Are the worries of tomorrow keeping you
awake? Remember—tomorrow is an opportunity to begin anew with your heavenly
Father. Seek Him, right now, through studying His Word and through prayer.
Embrace the promise that His compassion is new every morning. Great is His
faithfulness!

Lord, I'm so undeserving, but still You give and give and give.
Thank You for Your faithfulness.

MEMORY VERSE OF THE DAY

"Yet even now," declares the LORD, "return to Me with all your heart, and with fasting, weeping and mourning; and rend your heart and not your garments."

JOEL 2:12–13 NASB

Morning

HE RESTORES MY RIGHTEOUSNESS.

When you stray from God's path of righteousness, He asks that you to return to Him with a contrite heart, mind, and soul. His abundant love does more than patch a heart ripped open by regret. His mercy restores it. You are His, patched and mended, because of His great love for you.

Father God, I've made a mess of things. Please forgive me, and help me not to do it again!

Evening

HE FORGIVES ME.

To the early Israelites, ripping their garments indicated deep regret. The Lord asked them to rend their hearts; symbolizing the most profound remorse possible, accompanied by fasting, weeping, and mourning. Thanks to Jesus, you don't have to do that. All you need is to ask for God's forgiveness, and it's yours!

Dear Jesus, thank You for providing my path to forgiveness. Every day, I am grateful to You.

MEMORY VERSE OF THE DAY

*Do not let this one fact escape your notice, beloved, that with the Lord
one day is like a thousand years, and a thousand years like one day.*

2 Peter 3:8 nasb

Morning

GOD CREATED TIME.

Two thousand years have passed since Peter wrote about Christ's anticipated
return. But it's only been a day in heaven, maybe two. We can't comprehend God's
calendar. Infinity is a mystery. Although God dwells in eternity, He created time for
us here on earth. So, make the most of your time today.

*Lord, time is Your precious gift.
Remind me to make the most of it today.*

Evening

SAVE THE DATE?

You can't save the date for Christ's return because no one but God knows when
that will be. When that day comes, unlike anticipated happy occasions here on
earth, this glorious event won't be over in a flash. We will join the King of kings, in
a beautiful day that will last forever.

*Come, Lord Jesus! I look forward to that glorious day
when I will be with You forever.*

MEMORY VERSE OF THE DAY

"Whoever believes in me, as Scripture has said,
rivers of living water will flow from within them."

JOHN 7:38 NIV

Morning

LIVING WATER.

Moving water has the power to shape rocks, mountains, and valleys. Today's memory verse says that Christ within you is a continual, unstoppable force of living water, molding you, feeding you, directing you, and putting a spring of joy in your step! Walk joyfully today with God at Your side.

Today, Jesus, I will remember that You dwell within me.
Guide me. Teach me.

Evening

A POWERFUL PROMISE.

John 7:38 is one of those powerful promises from God. Whenever you take a drink of water, remember the living water that lies within you. Then allow Christ's power and love to flow out of you and into the lives of others. Keep that water flowing, and it can change the world!

Jesus, quench my thirst. Fill me with Your living water.

MEMORY VERSE OF THE DAY

"Do to others as you would like them to do to you."

LUKE 6:31 NLT

Morning

I WILL DO UNTO OTHERS.

Today's scripture verse is also known as the Golden Rule. What a wonderful world this would be if everyone treated others like they'd want to be treated. Such a movement can become a reality, and it can begin with you. Follow this Golden Rule today, and see how it makes you feel.

Help me to follow Your Golden Rule, Lord!

Evening

GOOD DEEDS ABOUND!

There's a million ways to share the riches found in the Golden Rule. Tonight, meditate on Luke 6:31. Then plan to do a good deed, or two, or three—or more! Jesus never ran out of ways to do good deeds for others. Make a list of what you might do. And then, do it!

Jesus, fill me up with all sorts of good deeds that I can do for others.
I'm ready! Let's go!

MEMORY VERSE OF THE DAY

*"For those who exalt themselves will be humbled,
and those who humble themselves will be exalted."*

MATTHEW 23:12 NIV

Morning

AWAY WITH YOU, PRIDE!

We talk about humility, but do we live it? No one sets out to be prideful, but it's difficult not to put personal needs and desires first. Still, when we humble ourselves and focus on others, God lifts us up. He does a far better job of exalting than we could ever do!

*God, forgive me for those times when I have been prideful.
I come to You now with a humble heart.*

Evening

DON'T STEAL THE SPOTLIGHT.

Are you guilty of drawing too much attention to yourself? Maybe you tend to over-share the positive, joyous things in your life, even when others around you are hurting. Maybe it's time to trim back a bit! When you turn the spotlight off of "self," God is free to shine at His finest!

*Make me aware, Father, when I am putting the "spotlight"
on myself instead of on You.*

MEMORY VERSE OF THE DAY

Do not let sin have power over you.
Let good have power over sin!

ROMANS 12:21 NLV

Morning

GOOD WINS OVER EVIL.

As a believer, you might argue that you are rarely "overcome" by sin and evil. However, there are days when your temper gets the best of you or you get overwhelmed. That's how the enemy catches you off guard and pulls you off course. Today, be aware of his tactics. Be prepared.

Open my eyes, Lord, to sin, and help me to fight it at every turn.

Evening

CALL IT WHAT IT IS.

Sometimes, we don't want to think about sneaky sin. We're scared of facing and fighting it. It's time to look it in the eye and call it what it is. Only then can you overcome its grip on you. Once you release your hold, you're in a position for good to truly win over evil.

I'm ready, Father, to admit my sin to You.
I know that You forgive me and will help me to fight it.

MEMORY VERSE OF THE DAY

Commit to the LORD whatever you do,
and he will establish your plans.

PROVERBS 16:3 NIV

Morning

GOD IS MY ARCHITECT.

God is the great architect of your life, and He has a custom life-plan just for you. Allowing Him to plan your life is never a risk, because He already knows exactly what you need. That was established even before you were born. God's plan is perfect for you.

Lord, help me not to get in the way of Your work.
I'm eager to see what You have planned for me.

Evening

I SURRENDER.

When you surrender control of your life to God, He takes even the minor details and molds them into a complete picture of what your life was meant to be. With God guiding your steps, the events in your life are never mere accidents. Each one has a purpose designed specifically for you.

I surrender control of my life to You, God. Take it.
Design it for Your glory.

MEMORY VERSE OF THE DAY

It is good for me that I have been afflicted, that I may learn Your statutes.
PSALM 119:71 NKJV

Morning

SHOULD I PLAY IT SAFE?

Everything has gone according to your plans. You face no resistance to what you want for your life because you've played it safe and taken no risks, eliminating any possibility of discomfort. But—think about it—we grow when we take risks and experience roadblocks. God uses them to deepen our faith.

Father God, it's easy to be comfortable where I'm at,
but where do You want me to go?

Evening

RISKY BUSINESS.

God uses affliction to sharpen your dependence on Him and prove His faithfulness. When you shield yourself so heavily from change or difficulties, you end up with a shallow faith. You are better off risking your peaceful safety in exchange for a depth of maturity that comes from taking well-calculated risks.

Dear God, open my eyes to risks worth taking;
then give me the courage to take them.

MEMORY VERSE OF THE DAY

Love from the center of who you are; don't fake it. Run for dear life from evil; hold on for dear life to good. Be good friends who love deeply; practice playing second fiddle.

ROMANS 12:9–10 MSG

Morning

LOVE WITH A GENUINE HEART.

The Message uses the metaphor, "practice playing second fiddle," to help us understand how we should honor one another. We should take the second part, putting others before ourselves, encouraging them with love and devotion. If you love without hypocrisy and honor others above yourself, you will help make the world a better place.

Dear Lord, please help me to love with a genuine heart and to take second place to those around me.

Evening

SOMETIMES, LOVE IS HARD.

It's easy to love some people, but how easy is it to love a person you just can't relate to? Being polite is one thing, but truly loving that person is much harder. God says we sin against Him when we pretend to love others but dislike them. He calls us to genuine love.

Heavenly Father, help me to love that difficult person in my life.

MEMORY VERSE OF THE DAY

*"This vision is for a future time. It describes the end,
and it will be fulfilled. If it seems slow in coming, wait patiently,
for it will surely take place. It will not be delayed."*

HABAKKUK 2:3 NLT

Morning

GOD, I'M WAITING.

What are you waiting for today? Sometimes the things you're waiting for might come slowly. Similarly, God's plans might come slowly, but they come steadily, surely. God is going to do what He says He'll do. You won't know when, exactly, but God wants you to be faithful while you wait.

*Lord, I'm used to things moving really fast.
Help me to wait patiently and faithfully.*

Evening

SLOWLY, STEADILY, SURELY.

Patience. It's the stuff frustration is made of. And yet it's a virtue the Lord expects His people to have plenty of. Take another look at today's scripture. Is your patience wearing thin? Learn the value of slowing down. Apply the slowly, steadily, surely principle, and watch God work—in His time.

Remind me daily, God, that Your timetable is the only one that matters.

MEMORY VERSE OF THE DAY

*"Call to me and I will answer you. I'll tell you marvelous
and wondrous things that you could never figure out on your own."*

JEREMIAH 33:3 MSG

Morning

GOD HAS ALL THE ANSWERS.

Where can you go to find answers to your deepest questions? When you need discernment, wisdom, or insight into a situation, God is never farther than a prayer away. He, the source of all knowledge, will give you the inside scoop. He'll tell you things you never imagined. That's divine inspiration!

I come to You in prayer, Lord, seeking Your knowledge. Fill me up!

Evening

HE GUIDES MY RELATIONSHIPS.

God answers your relationship questions, too. Some people may come and go in your life. But God will never desert you. His name is Immanuel—"God with us"— and He will never let go of you. He'll always be there to encourage and guide you through relationships and everything else.

Lead me, Lord. Guide me through this maze called life.

MEMORY VERSE OF THE DAY

You will. . .clear out the old [to make room] for the new.

LEVITICUS 26:10 AMP

 Morning

IS IT TIME TO MOVE ON?

There are times when something you once loved doing seems more like a burden than a blessing. It may be time to relinquish the old and begin a new endeavor. But, as in all things, before making that decision, ask the Lord for guidance. He'll steer you in the right direction.

Father, I've become weary of _____. Guide me.
Shall I stick with it or start something new?

Evening

WHAT DOES GOD WANT?

When you accepted Jesus, God gave you a new heart—a heart full of love for Him. Listen to your heart. Is God calling you to a new ministry for Him? A ministry can be anything that draws attention to Him, either directly or through example. What is God calling You to do?

God, are You wanting me to do something new for You?
Open my heart to hear You.

MEMORY VERSE OF THE DAY

"For God did not send his Son into the world to condemn the world, but in order that the world might be saved through him."

JOHN 3:17 ESV

Morning

NO COMMENT.

You will make mistakes (We all do.) but God doesn't stand over you, clucking His tongue and saying, "Can't you get anything right?" When you come to Him, accepting His gift of salvation, all of the icky stuff (worthy of critique) is washed away. There's nothing left to comment on!

O, Father God, thank You for forgiving me and washing away my sins.

Evening

I WILL FORGIVE MYSELF.

Don't be so hard on yourself. We all break God's heart with our actions. But even then, He gently woos us back with His amazing love and then pours out grace and mercy. Condemnation is a thing of the past when you walk with Him. So forgive yourself like He forgives you.

Lord, I need to forgive myself for past sins, and move on.
Will You help me to do that, please?

MEMORY VERSE OF THE DAY

Be happy in the Lord.
And He will give you the desires of your heart.

PSALM 37:4 NLV

 Morning ────────────────────────────

GOD CARES ABOUT WHAT I WANT.

God cares very much about the desires of your heart. He longs to see you giddy with delight over the blessings He can bestow. So, if you really want to benefit from all that the Lord has in store, make up your mind to be happy/content, no matter what.

Almighty Father, as I go about my work today,
fill my heart with happiness.

Evening ────────────────────────────

I AM HAPPY IN THE LORD.

When you are content "happy in the Lord" (as today's memory verse suggests) He will give you the desires of your heart. If you walk around unhappy all the time, grumbling and complaining, those blessings might be a little slower in coming. Strive to be happy. That's the best way to live.

God, when I feel like complaining,
remind me that You are my source of happiness—always!

MEMORY VERSE OF THE DAY

*Since God chose you to be the holy people he loves, you must clothe
yourselves with tenderhearted mercy, kindness,
humility, gentleness, and patience.*

COLOSSIANS 3:12 NLT

Morning

PUT ON YOUR GODLY CLOTHES!

Think about the attributes of God outlined in today's verse. It's your responsibility to put on this "godly attire" every morning. As you get dressed, you can intentionally decide to wear His attributes so others can see those qualities that characterize God's holiness—and by extension the qualities He graces you with, as well.

*Lord, I will dress myself this morning in tenderhearted mercy,
kindness, humility, gentleness, and patience.*

Evening

GOD WANTS ME TO BE HOLY.

God has chosen you for many things, but your highest calling is holiness—perhaps the hardest calling to fulfill. You cannot be holy on your own, because the world is not attracted to your own righteousness, which is flawed. Others can only detect holiness in the reflection of God working within you.

*Lord God, lift me up toward holiness,
by helping me to be a reflection of You.*

MEMORY VERSE OF THE DAY

Don't worry about anything; instead, pray about everything.
Tell God what you need, and thank him for all he has done.

PHILIPPIANS 4:6 NLT

Morning ————————————————————

DON'T WORRY ABOUT IT.

"Don't worry about it." How many times have you heard that? Don't worry. It's easier said than done. But, that is exactly what God wants you to do. When you put aside your worries, believing that He has everything under control, You show your faith in Him, and He will reward you.

God, I know that you have my problems under control,
so please, help me not to worry.

Evening ————————————————————

SAY THANK YOU!

When God fixes whatever it is you worried about, do you remember to thank Him? We teach our little ones to say thank you, but we sometimes ignore that practice in our relationship with God. Why does God want us to have a thankful heart? Because it gives Him the glory that He deserves.

O, Father, thank You for fixing my problems.
The glory is Yours, Lord. You can fix anything!

MEMORY VERSE OF THE DAY

Catch for us the foxes, the little foxes that ruin the vineyards.
SONG OF SOLOMON 2:15 NIV

Morning

AWAY WITH YOU, LITTLE FOXES!

The Bible teaches that the "little foxes" in life "spoil the vine." Little foxes are the trivial, petty annoyances you encounter daily. One or two consecutive foxes can hurl you into an all-out tailspin, ruining an otherwise perfect day. So, watch out for those little foxes today, and shoo them away.

Dear God, please give comfort to my disquieted soul
and drive away the little foxes of aggravation.

Evening

PRAYER + PRAISE= PEACE.

So how do we harness little foxes? The answer is simple: Prayer plus praise equals peace. God understands your human frailty. Wherever you are, whatever you are doing, He is eager to administer calm, peace, and joy! When you turn to God in prayer and praise, He begins to catch the foxes for you.

Father, when I'm tempted to fret and fume, remind me that prayer
and praise will keep my emotions in balance.

MEMORY VERSE OF THE DAY

Our bodies. . .were made for the Lord,
and the Lord cares about our bodies.

1 CORINTHIANS 6:13 NLT

Morning

GOD CARES ABOUT MY HEALTH.

Your body is a temple of the Most High God! He cares about how you take care of—or neglect—yourself. Today, be mindful of how you rest, work, eat, move, and play. Begin to sense what things are beneficial to your overall health and to the maintenance of your body—God's temple.

Lord, make me aware today of how I care for my body.
Help me to remember that it is Your temple.

Evening

MY BODY BELONGS TO HIM.

God's Word says that if you belong to the Lord, your body is not your own. God lives in you. Think about it: How do your daily choices affect your body? Are you stressed? Do your food choices leave much to be desired? Do you exercise? Vow to take better care of God's temple.

God, thank You for the gift of my body.
Help me to be a good steward of that gift.

MEMORY VERSE OF THE DAY

*Now may the Lord of peace Himself continually grant you peace
in every circumstance. The Lord be with you all!*

2 THESSALONIANS 3:16 NASB

Morning

GOD'S GIFT OF PEACE.

One of God's greatest gifts to humankind is peace. And it is yours for the asking.
In every trial and amid all life's traumas, peace will reign in your mind, body, and
soul if you are abiding in Jesus. Remain in Him and all will be well. Think about
that today.

Dear God, fill me with Your abundant, life–giving peace.

Evening

PRAY FOR PEACE.

Before you sleep tonight, pray for peace within your heart and in the world. Pray
for peace in your family, your community, in your church, and your workplace. Ask
God to bring peace into every circumstance. Then trust that He will provide—in
His own time. Believe it! Peace is coming.

*Jesus, when the world seems void of peace, remind me that You came
to bring peace to the world—and You are coming again. Come, Lord Jesus!*

MEMORY VERSE OF THE DAY

*So roll up your sleeves, put your mind in gear, be totally ready
to receive the gift that's coming when Jesus arrives.*

1 PETER 1:13 MSG

Morning

GET READY.

Recognizing that your future is in God gives you holy hope, determination, and confidence. When you allow Him to pull you into a life that is energetic, wise, and wholesome, all worldly troubles fade and you are remade! Get ready. Jesus is coming. Live in a way that's pleasing to Him.

*God, pull me into a life that is wholesome,
energetic, wise, and pleasing to You.*

Evening

BE PREPARED.

The best way to prepare for Jesus' coming is to learn what's in the Bible and apply it to your life. Scripture memorization isn't always easy, but you need to do it. It gets you ready for God's gift of eternal life. So, roll up your sleeves and commit more verses to memory!

*Jesus, help me to set my mind on the importance of memorizing
scripture so I will be prepared when You arrive.*

MEMORY VERSE OF THE DAY

Now godliness with contentment is great gain.

1 TIMOTHY 6:6 NKJV

Morning

WHAT IS CONTENTMENT?

To be content means you've settled an issue in your heart and don't spend your days wishing and hoping for things you don't have. Longings and desires don't drive you to feel like you're somehow missing out on "the good life." God has already given you the best possible life through His Son.

Dear heavenly Father, thank You for the gift of a contented life through Jesus!

Evening

ETERNAL LIFE IS MINE.

Eternal life is yours, bought and paid for by Jesus! And check it out! One day you will live in a mansion and walk on streets of gold. Wow! In the meantime, godly contentment will go a long way in preparing you for the bliss you will one day experience beyond heaven's pearly gates.

O, how wonderful, God, to know the riches that await me in heaven.
I love You!

MEMORY VERSE OF THE DAY

He will be great and will be called the Son of the Most High;
and the Lord God will give Him the throne of His father David.

LUKE 1:32 NASB

Morning

JESUS CHANGED EVERYTHING.

Jesus changed everything. Think about that today. The little baby in the manger changed history, changed the course of the church, and has changed your very life. Your family will never be the same. The world will never be the same. God's people will never be the same. . .and all because of Jesus.

Thank You, Jesus. Thank You for changing the world.

Evening

IS HE STILL CHANGING THINGS?

"Is Jesus still changing things today?" The answer is a resounding "Yes!" Invite Him to be the very center of the "thing" (relationship, problem, issue) you're facing. From that pivotal spot, Jesus is free to blow the winds to a completely different direction. Keep Him in His rightful place, then watch change come.

Lord Jesus, be at the center of my every thing,
and bring positive changes in all situations.

MEMORY VERSE OF THE DAY

*"For the life of every living thing is in his hand,
and the breath of every human being."*

JOB 12:10 NLT

Morning

I AM IN HIS HANDS.

Think about this: Is there a better place to be than in God's hands? With Him you can survive even the most horrendous circumstances. You are joined with Him at the very core of your being. His spirit and yours work together to bring you through the difficulties in life.

*Lord, You hold me gently because I am small and vulnerable.
Thank You for keeping me safe in Your hands.*

Evening

MY UNION WITH HIM IS REAL.

Tonight, meditate on your relationship with God. Your union with Him is more than just a casual relationship, and it adds to your life more than just superficial joy. When you live in Him, a godly life, then others see God in you, and suddenly your union with Him becomes real.

*Father, You and I have a special, unbreakable bond.
Reveal Yourself through me so others will see You and live.*

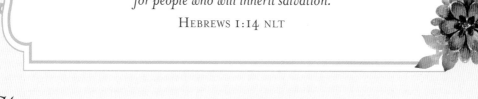

MEMORY VERSE OF THE DAY

Angels are only servants—spirits sent to care
for people who will inherit salvation.

HEBREWS 1:14 NLT

Morning

ANGELS WATCH OVER ME.

If God hasn't already provided you with all the help and protection you'll ever need, He also sends His angels to care for you. Though you can't see them, they are there, a constant presence in your life, sent by the Father to watch over you. Feel their presence today.

Angels, Lord! Angels constantly watching over me.
What a wonderful gift!

Evening

HIS ANGELS SERVE ME.

God surrounds you with a team of angels whose mission is to serve you. He instructs them to do His will concerning you. This is how important you are to Him: even the angels know how much He loves you. They are already standing guard over you. Remember that tonight as you fall asleep.

I feel peaceful, heavenly Father,
knowing that I will sleep with Your angels surrounding my bed.

MEMORY VERSE OF THE DAY

I bless God every chance I get;
my lungs expand with his praise.

PSALM 34:1 MSG

Morning

GOD LONGS TO HEAR MY PRAISE.

How can you develop a spirit of praise today? First, amp up your prayer time. Then throughout the day, find new reasons to offer thanks to the Father: the refreshment of a hot shower, food to satisfy hunger, the smile of a friend, the change of seasons. . .the list is endless!

Father I praise You for this new day.
Open my eyes to endless reasons to thank You.

Evening

SAY IT OUT LOUD!

Sprinkle your conversations with the hope that your faith gives. Verbally acknowledge God's goodness and provision in your life and in the lives of others. Call a coincidence what it really is—the hand of the Father. Don't be afraid to let your newfound praise bubble over to every area of your life!

Almighty God, I praise You for being You!
Let everything within me praise the Lord!

MEMORY VERSE OF THE DAY

Be still, and know that I am God:
I will be exalted among the heathen,
I will be exalted in the earth.

PSALM 46:10 KJV

 Morning ───────────────────

THERE IS STRENGTH IN STILLNESS.

God is found in stillness. Here is another verse to remember: "In returning and rest shall ye be saved; in quietness and in confidence shall be your strength" (Isaiah 30:15 KJV). God says stillness is good for you. It is how you come to know Him and gain your strength from Him.

Lord, I will find time to be still during my busy day.
I trust that in stillness You will renew my strength.

Evening ───────────────────

I WILL BE QUIET.

For many people stillness and quiet don't happen until they fall asleep, and they fall asleep with their minds still jabbering. Is that you? God never slumbers nor sleeps. Tonight, clear your head and be still. Sit quietly, eyes closed. Trust God to meet you in the pause. Listen to Him speak.

I will be still, Lord. I want Your voice to be the only one that I hear.

MEMORY VERSE OF THE DAY

Don't be misled—you cannot mock the justice of God.
You will always harvest what you plant.

GALATIANS 6:7 NLT

Morning

SEEDS OF THE SPIRIT.

One of God's spiritual laws is that you reap what you sow. Are you planting seeds of the spirit—such as love, forgiveness, and mercy? Or seeds of the flesh—hate, unforgiveness, and apathy? Work in the spirit and you will reap God's riches—now and forever! Sow good seeds today.

Lord of the Harvest, help me to sow the right seeds.

Evening

WHO IS GOD? I WANT TO KNOW.

One of the great benefits of memorizing scripture is learning about God's character. As you read about Him and strive to be more like Him, you give a powerful boost to those spiritual "seeds." Wherever you "plant" them, others will admire their beauty—they'll want some "God seeds" of their own!

Father, I want to know You even better.
Show Yourself to me through Your Word.

MEMORY VERSE OF THE DAY

Just as water mirrors your face,
so your face mirrors your heart.

PROVERBS 27:19 MSG

Morning

LOOK IN THE MIRROR.

Have you looked at yourself in the mirror lately? If so, do you like what you see? If not, check for a deeper source. Ask God to help you look into your heart and mind and reflect upon what you see. Work on that inner beauty, and your outer self will become simply gorgeous!

Search my heart and mind, Lord.
Give me insight into my soul.

Evening

THAT BEAUTIFUL GLOW.

Ads for cosmetics sometimes promise a "beautiful glow." But can they deliver on their promise? Not always. Makeup may hide the flaws, but they still exist. Inner beauty is different. When your heart overflows with God's love, you will have a beautiful glow always—it's a promise you can count on.

God, I want to glow with inner beauty!
Fill up my heart with You!

MEMORY VERSE OF THE DAY

Whoever conceals their sins does not prosper,
but the one who confesses and renounces them finds mercy.
PROVERBS 28:13 NIV

Morning

GOD IS MERCIFUL.

Sometimes we "sneak" a sinful action into our routine when we think no one is looking. But God is always looking, and our transgressions break His heart. Confessing our sin to Him isn't easy. Still, it's the only way to receive His mercy. Be careful about sin today. It can be sneaky.

Father God, sometimes I allow sin into my life.
Please have mercy on me.

Evening

CONFESSION IS GOOD FOR THE SOUL.

You've probably heard the expression: confession is good for the soul. Maybe it made no sense. To you, "confessing" meant getting in trouble. Aren't you glad you can safely confess your sins to God and receive grace and mercy in exchange? Confess your sins to Him tonight. He's waiting to forgive you.

God, I feel safe confessing my sins to You,
because I know that You love and will forgive me.

MEMORY VERSE OF THE DAY

*"Therefore, my friends, I want you to know that through Jesus
the forgiveness of sins is proclaimed to you."*

ACTS 13:38 NIV

 Morning

HE WASHES AWAY MY SINS.

Have you seen a waterfall rushing over rocks, plummeting to the stream below?
Then you have a good analogy of the "washing away" of sins. When you come to
God with a repentant heart, He takes your sins and throws them into the water.
Into the racing stream they go, never to be seen again.

*Thank You for washing away my sins,
Lord—washing them away forever.*

Evening

BELIEVE IT!

If you're struggling to believe you've been forgiven, picture those sins plummeting
into the rushing waters and then finally disappearing downstream. They're gone
forever. Trust that! What joy to know that God has washed you clean. You rise up
as a new creation in Him. That's the best promise of all!

*Dear God, fill me with the joy that comes from Your forgiveness.
Help me believe that my sins are gone forever.*

MEMORY VERSE OF THE DAY

*Immediately he spoke to them and said,
"Take courage! It is I. Don't be afraid."*

MARK 6:50 NIV

Morning

HE'S HERE!

Learning to recognize Jesus' presence helps you trust Him and have the assurance that you can accomplish what He asks. You come to know His ways and sense His guidance as you spend more time with Him. You discover that He wants to walk beside you every day. Focus on His presence today.

*Jesus, as You walk with me today, let me sense Your being.
I know that You are right here with me.*

Evening

JESUS IS MY COURAGE.

When you open your spiritual eyes to see Jesus working in you, you find courage, confidence, and motivation. Jesus dispels the darkness and lights your path so you won't give in to fear or lies. You don't have to worry about your deficiencies, because you are depending on Him. You have His courage inside you!

*O, Jesus, I need courage to face the trials in my life.
Remind me that I already have Your courage within me.*

MEMORY VERSE OF THE DAY

If your gift is to encourage others, be encouraging.

ROMANS 12:8 NLT

Morning

I WILL BE AN ENCOURAGER.

You can be an encourager even if encouragement is not your special gift. Encouragement flows from the love of Christ living in you, giving you the power to strengthen God's people. It doesn't take much; a smile, some encouraging words, or simply your presence in a time of need. Be an encourager today.

Father, who in my life needs encouragement today?
Help me to meet their need.

Evening

WE ALL NEED ENCOURAGEMENT.

Why is encouragement so important? Everyone needs extra comfort and new perspectives amid the harsh realities of today's world. Encouragement helps ease the pain and suffering that too many people live with. Look for opportunities to encourage. Ask God to teach you to be a good encourager. Practice it every day.

God, teach me the art of encouragement.
Then give me opportunities to practice it in my daily life.

MEMORY VERSE OF THE DAY

He comforts us in all our troubles so that we can comfort others.
When they are troubled, we will be able to give them
the same comfort God has given us.

2 CORINTHIANS 1:4 NLT

Morning

GOD THE COMFORTER.

God is the greatest source of comfort the human spirit will ever encounter. Think of those times when He has comforted you. Using that example, comfort others in His name. Who in your life could use some comfort today? Offer it in any small way that you are able.

Lord Jesus, sometimes it is difficult to know how to comfort someone.
Guide me. Show me what to do or say.

Evening

HOW CAN I HELP?

God wants you to reach out to others who face the same challenges you have faced. There is something special about the empathetic comfort of someone who has been in your situation. Do you know someone who is facing a familiar trial? Reach out to them. Listen. Encourage them. Don't be afraid.

Heavenly Father, _____ is facing the same problem I faced.
How can I help to comfort her/him? Show me.

MEMORY VERSE OF THE DAY

The LORD God Almighty will be with you,
just as you say he is.

AMOS 5:14 NIV

Morning

HE NEVER LEAVES ME.

When you have trouble feeling God's presence, you might ask, "Where are You, God?" Don't let the enemy tell you that God is not with you! God is near. Each day, tell yourself the truth: that He is always with you; then He "will be with you, just as you say he is."

Almighty One, I will seek You today.
Give me the sense of Your being all around me.

Evening

SAY IT, AND BELIEVE IT.

During those times when you don't sense God's presence, take a look around. See where you are. Look into the goodness of His Word. Seek His face. Don't let Him out of your sight. Proclaim that He is standing there, right by your side. And there He will be, just as you have said.

O, God, I know that You are right here by my side—
and there You will always be!

MEMORY VERSE OF THE DAY

Guard your heart above all else,
for it determines the course of your life.

PROVERBS 4:23 NLT

Morning

GET RID OF NEGATIVE THOUGHTS.

This morning, take an inventory of your thoughts. Are there more negative than positive ones? Imagine a broom sweeping away all the negative thoughts. Then replace them with the positive verses you have memorized. Those verses will freshen and beautify your newly clean "house" like a bouquet of flowers. That's heart smart!

Lord, help me to recall all the positive scriptures I have
memorized and to dwell on them today.

Evening

I WILL GUARD MY HEART.

When you feel defeated, confused, or harassed, chances are you are letting negative thoughts overpower God's powerful, positive promises. Guard your heart! Gird your mind with the truth from God's Word, and store it in your heart. Then your heart will soar, and your life will get back on the right course.

Help me guard my heart, Lord. Plant Your words inside
my heart and bring them ever to my mind.

MEMORY VERSE OF THE DAY

"Most assuredly, I say to you, he who hears My word and believes in Him who sent Me has everlasting life, and shall not come into judgment, but has passed from death into life."

JOHN 5:24 NKJV

Morning ——————————————————————————

FOREVER IS—FOREVER!

Have you contemplated the word *forever*? It's the kind of word that leaves your head spinning. Sure, you can read those "happily ever after" books and wonder about a limited view of forever, but God's version of forever goes on, well— forever! Into eternity. Beyond the limitations of your calendar. Think about it.

Father, I hold tight to Your promise of eternity.
I can only imagine how wonderful it will be.

Evening ——————————————————————————

I CAN LIVE FOREVER.

God's word gives you glimpses of heaven. It's going to be blissful! If you've accepted Jesus as Lord of your life, then eternity began the moment you said, "I do!" to your Savior. You're already walking toward eternity. You are destined to live forever. The joy of expecting heaven has begun.

Dear Jesus, thank You for the gift of salvation and for
the assurance of eternal life in heaven.

MEMORY VERSE OF THE DAY

*Command those who are rich in this present world not to be arrogant
nor to put their hope in wealth, which is so uncertain,
but to put their hope in God.*

1 TIMOTHY 6:17 NIV

Morning

THINK ETERNALLY.

How much do you trust in worldly things? Remember that things are not forever.
What you own represents much less than God wants for you. Things don't have
power to change you. They only keep you tied to the physical world. So, today, get
into the habit of thinking eternally.

*Dear Lord, when I get too wrapped up in wanting some worldly thing,
remind me to turn my thoughts toward You.*

Evening

REACH FOR GODLY INTANGIBLES.

The spiritual activity in your life is what brings abundance, security, and
permanence. If you reach for godly intangibles like holiness, charity, and wisdom,
you will move to a deeper level of existence—and that's something God wants you
to experience. Ask Him to strengthen your spiritual life in relationship with Him.

*Almighty God, help me to grow in holiness, wisdom, and charity.
Bring me into a deeper relationship with You.*

MEMORY VERSE OF THE DAY

The LORD's plans stand firm forever;
his intentions can never be shaken.

PSALM 33:11 NLT

Morning

GOD'S PLAN IS FIRM.

When your life seems to be crumbling all around you, remember that God's plan for you stands firm. He knows what you need and how to fix your brokenness, because His intentions toward you were formed before you were born. His plan is a better design than you could possibly invent for yourself.

Father, when my plans crumble, help me to remember that
Your plans for me are better. They cannot be broken.

Evening

GOD'S PLAN IS PERFECT.

God's plan for you isn't affected by your indecisiveness or reluctance to obey, nor is the way He deals with you when you refuse to listen. God's patience outlasts your disobedience. His plan for you is solid and perfect. So, put aside any resistance; welcome His plan for your life.

Lord, forgive me for resisting what You have planned for me.
I give You control, and I welcome Your plan.

MEMORY VERSE OF THE DAY

"If they obey and serve him, they will spend the rest of their days in prosperity and their years in contentment."

JOB 36:11 NIV

Morning

I WANT TO SERVE HIM.

Most of us love to be served. There's nothing wrong with being served, but the Bible makes it clear that listening to God's voice and then serving Him—with worship, kindness toward others, and so on—isn't just a good idea, it's a great idea! How will you serve Him today?

Lord, it's nice to be served, but today I want to serve You by serving others. Show me how.

Evening

HIS PROMISE TO ME.

God knows when you serve from your heart—not expecting anything in return. And when you do that, you are guaranteed something wonderful. Here is God's promise to you: when you serve Him, you will end your days in prosperity and pleasure. What a terrific way to wrap up your life!

O, Father, how grateful I am for Your promise to me. It is my pleasure to serve You. I worship and adore You!

MEMORY VERSE OF THE DAY

Do not cast me from your presence or take your Holy Spirit from me.
Restore to me the joy of your salvation and grant me
a willing spirit, to sustain me.

PSALM 51:11–12 NIV

Morning ────────────────────────

RESTORE MY JOY.

This world will do all it can to pull you down, to tell you to give up. When you're tempted to grow discouraged, remember that you stand in the presence of God, and that He has given you the gift of His Spirit for times such as these. Find joy in His company.

God, sometimes I feel overwhelmed and weary.
Please restore my spirit. Help me to feel joyful again.

Evening ────────────────────────

HELP ME TO PERSEVERE.

Ask God for the power to press forward when your spirit grows tired. Try turning to other Christian believers for encouragement. Know that you are not alone—that you will never be alone. God craves your devotion. Recognize your own strength in His eyes. Turn to Him, and He will help you persevere.

Help me to keep going, Father. Renew my strength,
and grant me a willing spirit.

MEMORY VERSE OF THE DAY

My people will live in a peaceful habitation,
and in secure dwellings and in undisturbed resting places.

ISAIAH 32:18 NASB

Morning

GOD HONORS A HAPPY HOME.

God wants your home to be peaceful and happy, and that begins with you. Put a smile on your face and speak to your family in a soft, positive, encouraging voice. You set the tone of your home, and you control the pace within it. Make it a place of peace today.

Lord, guide me today to create a peaceful and happy atmosphere at home.

Evening

BE PROACTIVE AND PEACEFUL.

It takes effort to leave the world's cares at the front door and stay committed to the pursuit of a peaceful home. Ask God to help you shake off the frustration of work, school, relational, and financial concerns. Make a decision to be proactive and peaceful instead of reactive and defensive.

Dear God, release me from the stresses of today,
and give me a gentle, encouraging attitude at home.

MEMORY VERSE OF THE DAY

Since God is on our side, who can be against us?

ROMANS 8:31 NIrV

Morning

GOD IS MY SUPERHERO.

There's no need to quiver and shake. You have the ultimate Superhero on your side! No one can harm you, for God is bigger, stronger, and mightier than any foe you may face. Simply shine the God-Signal across the Gotham City of your mind. He'll be there in a flash!

How wonderful that with You in my life, Lord,
nothing can prevail against me!

Evening

GOD IS REAL!

God is not like a fictitious superhero on a movie screen. God and His powers are real! And don't let anyone convince you otherwise. Believe that God exists and keep seeking His company. As you continue to walk and talk with Him, you will feel His presence all around you.

Dear God, even in those fleeting moments of unbelief,
I will hold tight to You and not let go.

MEMORY VERSE OF THE DAY

*They attacked me at a moment when I was in distress,
but the LORD supported me. He led me to a place of safety;
he rescued me because he delights in me.*

PSALM 18:18–19 NLT

Morning ——————————————————

GOD IS ON STANDBY.

When you are at your lowest, you may be easy prey, open to attack by the enemy. But don't worry. God is on standby, ready to lift you up out of trouble and set you down in a safe place. Why? Because He loves you! When you are weak, He is your strength!

Lord, thank You for always being there.

Evening ——————————————————

SLOW DOWN!

How tired are you? When you over-schedule and run yourself ragged, you are more open to distress and disease. Recall those scripture verses you have memorized about finding rest. God wants you to slow down and spend more time relaxing with Him by reading His Word and praying. Will you do that?

*Father God, I need to slow down. Help me to reprioritize my life
by putting You first and resting in Your love.*

DAY 188

MEMORY VERSE OF THE DAY

*You also, like living stones, are being built into a spiritual house
to be a holy priesthood, offering spiritual sacrifices
acceptable to God through Jesus Christ.*

1 PETER 2:5 NIV

Morning

I AM A LIVING STONE.

Today's scripture makes it clear that believers are "living" stones being built up into a spiritual house. Think about that. You are a living stone. Not brick and mortar—the stuff used to build an ordinary house. You're alive in Jesus, and not just while you're on earth, either. You're alive for eternity.

Thank You, Jesus, for giving me new life and the promise of eternal life in heaven.

Evening

A FOREVER KIND OF HOUSE.

The spiritual house that God is building is a forever kind of house. Termites won't tear it down. Wind and rain won't blow it over. It will stand the test of time. What is the purpose of this house? To offer up spiritual sacrifices/praises to the Lord. Your very life is a praise offering!

*God, I'm so grateful for Your promise of forever.
I praise You, Lord. I praise You!*

MEMORY VERSE OF THE DAY

Now it is God who makes both us and you stand firm in Christ.
He anointed us, set his seal of ownership on us, and put his Spirit
in our hearts as a deposit, guaranteeing what is to come.

2 Corinthians 1:21–22 NIV

Morning

JESUS SEALED THE DEAL.

To be "sealed" means there's no chance of destruction after the fact. God's seal is perfect and indestructible forever. Think about that for a moment. When Jesus died on the crossed, He "sealed the deal" for you. Nothing can "unseal" His eternal work on Calvary! He's even given you His Spirit as a pledge.

Thank You, Jesus, for "sealing the deal"
on that "house" waiting for me in heaven.

Evening

I AM HIS.

Nothing will change God's mind. You are His. And you don't need to fear "destruction" of any kind as long as you are sealed in Him. You are safe and secure, standing firm. He's put His Spirit in your heart as a deposit (promise) of what's to come. Meditate on that tonight.

O, Father, I feel safe and secure with Your Spirit in my heart.
I'm glad that I belong to You.

MEMORY VERSE OF THE DAY

*"I looked for someone among them who would build up the wall
and stand before me in the gap on behalf of the land so
I would not have to destroy it, but I found no one."*

EZEKIEL 22:30 NIV

 Morning

I WILL PRAY FOR OTHERS.

When you ask others to pray for you, you're counting on them to help carry you through the tough times. Do you give the same consideration to those who ask you for prayer? Remember, they are trusting you to stand in the gap for them during their difficult times. Who needs your prayers today?

*Father God, forgive me for not praying for everyone
who asks me for prayer. I will try to do better.*

Evening

DON'T DELAY.

Today's verse is about a man left without the prayers of others. Don't make someone else like him. Take time as soon as you receive a prayer request to talk to the Lord on the requester's behalf. Be the bridge that carries that person through the valley of darkness back to the mountaintop of joy.

*Heavenly Father, help me to have a heart of compassion for those I know
and even for those I don't know who need Your comfort and love.
Help me never to be too busy to pray for them.*

MEMORY VERSE OF THE DAY

*But they said. . ."You can't get in here!". . .But David went
right ahead and captured the fortress of Zion.*

2 SAMUEL 5:6–7 MSG

Morning

TUNNEL TO VICTORY.

David disregarded the naysayers, tunneled his way into Jerusalem, and overtook
the city! Follow his lead. Today, ignore the negative voices, keep alert for other
choices, and if the wall before you seems impregnable, keep searching for your
God-given path. Your heavenly Father will guide you to tunnel your way to victory.

I need a plan, Lord. Show me the way to victory.

Evening

SEEK GOD'S WISDOM.

When you begin endeavors without first seeking God's direction or approval,
previously unseen obstacles may rise up in your path. Remember this: God is the
source of all wisdom. Ask Him to help you stay focused on Him. Open yourself to
listen closely to and trust in His perfect wisdom and direction.

*Heavenly Father, when I run on ahead of You,
remind me to always seek You first, and You will direct my path.*

MEMORY VERSE OF THE DAY

Go to work in the morning and stick to it until evening without watching the clock. You never know from moment to moment how your work will turn out in the end.

ECCLESIASTES 11:6 MSG

Morning

I WILL STAY IN THE ZONE.

No matter what task you undertake today, get yourself into the zone. Resolve not to give in to thoughts like *What if this doesn't work out?* or *How am I ever going to manage this?* Close your eyes, say a prayer, and Let the Holy Spirit take control of your heart, hands, feet, and mind.

I don't know what today holds for me, Father, but I trust You.

Evening

JESUS IS WITH ME.

Jesus loves you and wants to spend time with you. He longs for your presence. Don't take Him for granted. Rise up tomorrow morning, and every morning. Run into His waiting arms. There lies peace, love, and contentment for the entire day. Sleep now, in the crook of His arm.

Thank You for all Your love, Jesus.
Where would I be without You?

MEMORY VERSE OF THE DAY

*Let the peace of Christ rule in your hearts, since as members
of one body you were called to peace. And be thankful.*

COLOSSIANS 3:15 NIV

Morning

PEACE RULES!

What does it mean to allow peace to "rule" your heart? In order for that to happen, you have to submit yourself to the process. You have to trust God completely, willingly approach Him, and say, "Father, I can't live in chaos and turmoil anymore." Will you do that today?

*Father, I give up. Please replace all the stress
in my heart with Your perfect peace.*

Evening

YES, I TRUST HIM!

After you make that commitment to allow peace to rule your heart, you must believe that God will flood your heart with His unmistakable peace *every* time you're tempted to get anxious. Can you live like that moment to moment? If you trust Him, yes! That is another of His wonderful promises!

*Heavenly Father, I trust You to flood my heart with Your peace.
Help me to trust even more!*

MEMORY VERSE OF THE DAY

*Accept one another, then, just as Christ accepted you,
in order to bring praise to God.*

ROMANS 15:7 NIV

Morning

GOD WON'T REJECT ME.

To be accepted means you don't have to work to earn God's love. There's nothing you can do to be "un-accepted" either. God won't reject you if you make mistakes. This is why God is so keen on us accepting one another (fellow believers) in love. No judging. No divisions. Just acceptance.

*Dear Lord, thank You for accepting me,
just the way I am, all the time. I love You!*

Evening

I WILL ACCEPT *ALL* BELIEVERS.

No, we don't all worship exactly the same way, but we serve the same heavenly Father and He longs for us to dwell together in unity. So, accept His love, and then accept your fellow believers as part of the family. In this way, you will show the Father's heart.

*Father God, help me to remember that all of us are Yours and
to accept those who worship You differently from me.*

MEMORY VERSE OF THE DAY

As a father has compassion on his children,
so the Lord has compassion on those who fear him.

PSALM 103:13 NIV

Morning ———————————————————————

MY GOD IS COMPASSIONATE.

How do you need God to show you His compassion today? Do you need guidance for a decision? Ask Him. He will show you what to do. Do you want someone to talk to? He is always available. Whatever you need today, forgiveness, help, wisdom—seek your compassionate Father. He loves you.

Father God, I'm so grateful for the blessing of Your eternal compassion.
You meet my every need.

Evening ———————————————————————

I WILL BE COMPASSIONATE, TOO!

Once you've experienced God's compassion, you'll want to share it with others. Ask God how you can be a blessing to someone. Does a coworker need encouragement? Could your best friend use some listening time? If you ask Him, God will give you fresh ideas on ministering compassion to those around you.

Lord, I am so thankful for—and in awe of—Your compassion.
Help me spread it to everyone I know.

MEMORY VERSE OF THE DAY

Cast your burden upon the LORD and He will sustain you;
He will never allow the righteous to be shaken.

PSALM 55:22 NASB

 Morning ——————————————————————

I WILL GIVE HIM MY BURDENS.

Do you always remember to take your burdens to the One who can do something about them? We are called to release our cares to our heavenly Father. A cause with an effect is implied in Psalm 55:22—If you cast your burden on Him, then He will sustain you. Think about it.

Father, I can't bear them alone any longer. In my weakness,
You are strong. Thank You for Your promise to sustain me.

Evening ——————————————————————

HE IS JUST A PRAYER AWAY.

Does it sound inviting to have the God of the universe strengthen and support you? Would it help if He bore the weight of your current trials? God is there when heartaches come. He doesn't have a cell phone or an e-mail address, but He is always just a prayer away.

Lord, please lift the worries that weigh on my mind and heart today.
Strengthen and sustain me.

MEMORY VERSE OF THE DAY

The Lord your God is in the midst of you. . . ! He will rejoice over you with joy. . .and in His love He will be silent and make no mention [of past sins, or even recall them].

ZEPHANIAH 3:17 AMPC

Morning —————————————————————————

GOLDEN SILENCE.

Remember this: God is watching you and knows every decision you make. But no matter what you do, He, unlike fellow humans, will never say, "I told you so!" Instead, He will rejoice over you and love you! How great He is! His silence about past sins is truly golden.

Thank You, God, for being silent about those sins I have confessed to You. Your forgiveness is forever.

Evening —————————————————————————

HE FORGIVES—AND FORGETS!

How wonderful it is when someone whom you have wronged not only forgives you, but never again mentions what you did—and not only that, but also forgets it! That is what God promises to do. Why? Because He loves you with a love that is pure, perfect, and true.

Great is Your faithfulness, Lord! You love me, rejoice over me, and remember my sins no more!

MEMORY VERSE OF THE DAY

*Though there are no sheep in the pen and no cattle in the stalls,
yet I will rejoice in the Lord.*

HABAKKUK 3:17–18 NIV

Morning

HE IS WHY I AM HAPPY.

Okay. So maybe things didn't go as you planned. Instead of wallowing in self-pity or fuming in frustration, praise the Lord for what has gone right in your life. Before you know it, you will have your focus where it belongs—on Him—and find your faith lifting you higher and higher.

I lift my voice and rejoice in You, O Lord!

Evening

POSITIVE THOUGHTS.

Are you able to think positive thoughts, even when things don't go your way? You can, if you try! Meditate on everything good that God has done for you. Make a list. Count up your blessings, and then praise God for them. If you do this every night, you will be thinking positively in no time!

*Dear God, I sometimes dwell on what's wrong instead of all that You do for me.
Forgive me, and thank You for Your many blessings!*

MEMORY VERSE OF THE DAY

He replied, "Because you have so little faith. Truly I tell you, if you have faith as small as a mustard seed, you can say to this mountain, 'Move from here to there,' and it will move. Nothing will be impossible for you."

MATTHEW 17:20 NIV

Morning ———————————————

HAVE A LITTLE FAITH!

Today's verse teaches that a tiny amount of faith is enough. Think of it as a seed, a starting point. You don't have to wait around until your faith grows. You can put it into action right now. So, what are you waiting for? Plant a little faith today, and watch it grow!

Almighty God, I have faith, if only just a little. Help me to act on my faith today and trust You.

Evening ———————————————

JESUS AND I, TOGETHER.

Maybe you long for—and hope to achieve—massive amounts of faith right away. Maybe you think that your puny amount of faith won't be enough to do great things. Jesus said that it *is* enough! He will take your small amount of faith, and together, you and He will move mountains.

Jesus, my faith is in You. Build it up; make it strong. There is nothing that You and I can't do!

MEMORY VERSE OF THE DAY

The LORD gives strength to his people;
the LORD blesses his people with peace.

PSALM 29:11 NCV

Morning ———————————————————

GOD–BREATHED STRENGTH.

God-breathed strength is the sort that invigorates you even on days when you feel you can't put one foot in front of the other. It's an inside-out strength. Do you need some God-breathed strength today? If so, acknowledge your need to your heavenly Father. Admitting your weakness is nothing to be ashamed of.

Father, I am so weak, and You are so strong.
Give me the strength I need today.

Evening ———————————————————

FATHER, I NEED YOUR HELP.

Admitting you can't handle something is a good thing because it frees God up to handle it for you. (Seriously. . .why would He intervene if you went around announcing that you had it all together?) Admit that you need help. Then watch as He gives you the strength to handle all you're facing.

Lord, this situation is too big for me to handle on my own.
Take it into Your capable hands, and help me.

MEMORY VERSE OF THE DAY

You were bought at a price.

1 CORINTHIANS 6:20 NIV

Morning

I AM A PERFECT FIT.

When it seems others do not want you on their team or you find you're having a hard time fitting in, remember you are part of God's family. He created you and formed you to be a perfect fit. No matter where you've been or what you've done, God has accepted you.

When I'm tempted to feel rejected or unwanted,
remind me that I don't have to look far to find my perfect place in You.

Evening

JESUS PAID IT ALL.

God is all about your future, and that includes spending eternity with Him. He shaped you to the perfect size to fit into His purpose and plan. And no matter what road you take, He has made a place for you. He purchased you with the price of His own Son's life.

Jesus, thank You for paying the ultimate price for me to be a part of Your family.

MEMORY VERSE OF THE DAY

He restoreth my soul:
he leadeth me in the paths of righteousnes
for his name's sake.

PSALM 23:3 KJV

Morning

HE RESTORES MY SOUL.

Feeling down today? Turn your thoughts and prayers toward God. Focus on a hymn or a praise song and play it in your mind. Praise chases away the doldrums. Thankfulness to the Father can turn your plastic smiles into real ones, and as the psalm states, your soul will be restored.

Father, I'm down in the dumps today. You are my unending
source of strength. Gather me in Your arms for always.

Evening

BE ENCOURAGED!

Still feeling a little down tonight? Be encouraged. The Lord has promised He hears your pleas and knows your situation. He will never leave you. Your God is not a God of negativity, but of possibility. He will guide you through your difficulties and beyond them. Talk with Him tonight.

O, Father, when I am down, I will trust You to lift me up.
Pour out Your love to me tonight.

MEMORY VERSE OF THE DAY

Little children, let us not love in word or talk but in deed and in truth.

I JOHN 3:18 ESV

Morning —————————————————

LOVE IN ACTION.

God doesn't just want you to read or talk about living a godly life. He wants you to get out there and live it. You can't grow a garden unless you get up and start sowing some seeds. So stop talking and start walking! Change your world with love in action.

Give me the courage to live Your Word, Jesus.

Evening —————————————————

GOD'S KIND OF LOVE.

How do you measure up as a loving spouse, friend, neighbor, or coworker? Loving-kindness is a good thing, but God's kind of love—perfectly true love—is even better. You'll learn about His kind of love in the Bible through examples of how He treated His people. Have you read your Bible today?

God, I want to love with a love that is pure and true—
Your kind of love! Show me how, please.

MEMORY VERSE OF THE DAY

His divine power has given us everything we need for a godly life through our knowledge of him who called us by his own glory and goodness.

2 PETER 1:3 NIV

Morning

JESUS GIVES ME ALL I NEED.

Today's memory verse is a reminder that Jesus has given you all you need to live the life He has called you to live. Reading the Word, gaining godly knowledge, feeds that divine power within you. Continue to learn of Him, and you will grow closer than you ever dared dream!

Lord, I want to learn more about You. Lead me through Your Word!

Evening

GOD, WHO DO YOU THINK I AM?

Memorizing scripture isn't enough. You need to meditate on it—really think about what it means to you. God uses His Word to speak directly to you. Maybe you have already gained insight into your life through verses you have memorized. Dig deeper. Grow in the knowledge of who You are in Him.

Dear God, I want a deeper knowledge of who You think I am. Speak to me through Your Word. Teach me.

MEMORY VERSE OF THE DAY

*See, I set before you today life and prosperity, death and destruction.
For I command you today to love the LORD your God, to walk in obedience
to him, and to keep his commands, decrees and laws; then you will live
and increase, and the LORD your God will bless you in the
land you are entering to possess.*

DEUTERONOMY 30:15–16 NIV

Morning

THE PROMISED LAND.

What "land" do you wish to possess? Perhaps you're longing for a lasting friendship or a new, working vehicle. Whatever you're waiting for, rest assured, God cares. He has blessed you to enter your "promised land" but the timing of that entrance is completely up to Him. Wait, and trust in Him.

*Havenly Father, help me to wait patiently for what I want.
Please get my thoughts in line with Your will.*

Evening

CHOICES. . .CHOICES.

God sets choices in front of you. When you listen to Him, it's easier to get His perspective when you face several options. In the meantime, you are to live according to His commands and decrees. When you do that, you will not only possess the land but be blessed along the way.

*Lord, You know what is best for me and the path I should take.
I will follow You willingly and obediently.*

MEMORY VERSE OF THE DAY

I sought the LORD, and He answered me,
and delivered me from all my fears.

PSALM 34:4 NASB

Morning

I WILL FACE MY FEARS.

Fear is the enemy's tool, and you can defeat it. How? By seeking God's help. Ask Him to help you be willing to acknowledge fear and bravely face it. This sounds easy, but when faced with crippling terror it is harder than you thought it would be. Trust! God *will* help you. Believe it!

> *Dear Jesus, I know that You will help me to face my fears.*
> *I believe that, and I trust You.*

Evening

FEAR, GET OUT!

Defeating fear means remembering that God is the One fighting the battles for you. He's the One taking control. Still, He expects your participation. So, take a deep breath. Look fear directly in the eyes and holler, "Get out of here!" at the top of your lungs. Then watch fear dash away!

> *Almighty God, I will stand strong against fear. I will not run.*
> *I know that You will fight this battle for me—and win!*

MEMORY VERSE OF THE DAY

You are all sons of God through faith in Christ Jesus.
GALATIANS 3:26 NASB

Morning

I AM HIS CHILD.

As a Christian, you are a child of the King of kings, the Lord of lords, the sovereign God. He is the One who hung the stars in the sky, and yet He knows the number of hairs on your head. You are not just God's friend or distant relative. You are His child!

Thank You, Father, for adopting me through Christ as Your child.
Teach me to live as a reflection of Your love.

Evening

WE ARE ALL ONE IN HIM.

Read Galatians 3:26-29. It is packed with statements about who we are as Christians: Abraham's seeds, heirs according to God's promise, and best of all—children of God. Galatians reminds us that there is no male or female, race, or social status in God's eyes. Believers are truly one in Him.

Father, thank You for my brothers and sisters in Christ.
Help me to see them all through Your eyes.

MEMORY VERSE OF THE DAY

That clinches it—help's coming, an answer's on the way,
everything's going to work out.

PSALM 20:6 MSG

Morning

GOD HAS THE PERFECT SOLUTION.

If you're going through a particularly stressful time, if you need answers and they don't seem to be coming, recommit yourself to trusting God. Don't try to figure things out on your own. Instead, trust in the King of kings, the Lord of lords, the One who created you. He has the perfect solution.

Father God, today I recommit myself to trusting—
not in myself or my own answers—but in You.

Evening

IT'S ALL GOING TO WORK OUT.

How do you deal with problems when they look like they couldn't possibly work out? Trust God. Sounds easy, but it's tough when you're facing the unknown without clear answers. Still, God wants you to remain faithful during these times, and to remember help is coming. It is! Everything is going to work out.

Lord, trust is hard when I can't seem to find the answers I need.
Thank You that Your answer is on its way.

MEMORY VERSE OF THE DAY

"For the eyes of the LORD range throughout the earth to strengthen those whose hearts are fully committed to him."

2 CHRONICLES 16:9 NIV

Morning

MY HEART IS COMMITTED TO HIM.

God is on a mission. He is constantly on the lookout for people who will perform His will. He's roaming the earth right now, and He's watching all your actions. Do a heart check. Is it fully committed to Him? If so, get ready! He's going to do a marvelous work through you!

I'm awaiting Your orders, Lord. Speak! Here I am!

Evening

I THINK AND ACT TO PLEASE HIM.

Do you anticipate God's blessings? You should! When you are faithfully dedicated to Him, always anticipating His blessings, He will rescue you from trouble. He will give you wisdom and put you in a position of power. Think and act to please God, and He'll think and act for you.

Lord, I am Your servant. Show me Your will.

MEMORY VERSE OF THE DAY

I will take care of you. I created you.
I will carry you and always keep you safe.

ISAIAH 46:4 CEV

Morning

GOD IS MY CAREGIVER.

Do you long for someone to care for you? God cares! He is with you from the time you were conceived to all the days beyond. God is your caregiver, familiar with every part of you. He will bear you up and surround you with His protection. Rejoice in His presence; feel His love!

I praise You, my Caregiver, my God.

Evening

I WILL ALLOW OTHERS TO HELP ME.

Maybe you are busy caring for a family member or friend. God understands the stress and difficulties you face. As you care for that someone else, remember that God cares for you. He gives you permission to do what you need most—allow *yourself* to accept caregiving from others. You deserve it!

Father, thank You for understanding me and caring for me.
When I think I can do it all by myself, help me to
accept tender loving care from others.

MEMORY VERSE OF THE DAY

"Ask, and it will be given to you; seek, and you will find; knock, and it will be opened to you. For everyone who asks receives, and he who seeks finds, and to him who knocks it will be opened."

MATTHEW 7:7–8 NKJV

Morning ——————————————

APPROACH HIM WITH BOLDNESS.

God wants you to approach Him boldly and to come to His throne room with a childlike sense of expectation. That is why He tells you to ask. To seek. To knock. Instead of timidly approaching your heavenly Father, you need to come into His presence with childlike anticipation.

*Dear God, thank You for being so open to my requests.
I am never afraid to approach You with my heart's desires.*

Evening ——————————————

KNOCK ON GOD'S DOOR.

Remember what you were like as a kid? You weren't afraid to ask for. . .anything! Knock on the door, child of God! Your Father is standing on the other side, ready to bless you. Ask Him for your heart's desire. Pray boldly tonight. Listen for His words in your heart.

*O, Father, how wonderful that Your door is always open
and You are inside waiting for me.*

MEMORY VERSE OF THE DAY

The name of the LORD is a strong fortress;
the godly run to him and are safe.

PROVERBS 18:10 NLT

Morning ———————————————————

JESUS IS MY SAFE PLACE.

Remember childhood games that involved a "base" (a safe place) you could run to? There is still a "base" that you can run to, one where you're completely and totally safe—from harm, from pain, from distress, from anything! That base is the Lord Jesus. Trust Him to keep you safe today.

Jesus, thank You for being my safe place to run to.
I know I am safe today, because You are with me.

Evening ———————————————————

I AM TRULY SAFE IN HIM.

Jesus is like a strong tower. If you think of it in fairy-tale terms, it's that high place where you look out over the kingdom, free from worries. You are a daughter of the King! So, run into the safety of His arms tonight. Don't wait. You can be truly safe in Him.

Dear Jesus, keep me safe tonight as I sleep.
Guard and watch over my household and me.

MEMORY VERSE OF THE DAY

*Now faith is confidence in what we hope for
and assurance about what we do not see.*

HEBREWS 11:1 NIV

Morning

WHAT I SEE IS NOT WHAT I GET!

What you see right now, how you feel, is not a picture of what your faith is producing. Your faith is active, and God is busy working to make all things come together and benefit you. In the same way, your faith works behind the scenes of your life to produce a God-inspired outcome to situations you face. What you see is not what you get when you walk by faith.

*Heavenly Father, what I see today is not what I'm going to get.
Thank You for working behind the scenes to bring about the very best for my life.*

Evening

GOD IS WORKING IT OUT.

Be encouraged tonight that no matter what takes place in the natural world—what you see with your eyes—it doesn't have to be the final outcome of your situation. If you've asked God for something, then you can trust that He is working out all the details behind the scenes. Be patient.

*God, things might not look good right now, but I trust that
You are working everything out, and the result will be awesome!*

MEMORY VERSE OF THE DAY

*So the cloud of the LORD was over the tabernacle by day,
and fire was in the cloud by night, in the sight of all
the Israelites during all their travels.*

EXODUS 40:38 NIV

Morning

HE LIGHTS MY WAY.

Rest assured, God will shine His light on your travels, just as He led the Israelites with a cloud by day and a fire by night. Allow Him to lead you. His guidance will be accompanied with peace, joy, and a certainty that you have followed One who has your best interests at heart.

*Faithful Father, I praise You for Your compassion
and concern for me. Go before me today. Lead me.*

Evening

CAN I DETERMINE GOD'S WILL?

How do you determine God's will for the path you should take? Pray for His guidance. Search His Word, and make sure your decision aligns with scripture. Seek counsel from godly advisers. And then listen to your heart. God will provide you with the wisdom you need for your decision. He will lead you!

O, Lord, guide me with Your holy light as I seek Your will for my life.

MEMORY VERSE OF THE DAY

*Peter asked Jesus, "What about him, Lord?" Jesus replied, "If I want
him to remain alive until I return, what is that to you?
As for you, follow me."*

JOHN 21:21–22 NLT

Morning

ON COURSE WITH THE SOURCE.

Remember this today: Jesus wants you to follow Him and not stick your nose into
assignments He's given to others. If the urge to be a ministry meddler strikes, turn
your eyes back to Jesus before you trip up. Get back on course with the Source.
Follow Him full force!

Jesus, I'm following right behind You—You are my Source and my Guide.

Evening

MIND YOUR OWN BUSINESS!

Today's memory verse reminds you to mind your own business. Sometimes, trying
to help when God is working out His plan in someone else's life only hinders the
progress. Pray tonight that His will be done for your brothers and sisters. Then
keep your eyes fixed on what He is doing in *your* life.

*Almighty Father, sometimes I slip up and meddle in others' lives.
Help me not to do that, please.*

MEMORY VERSE OF THE DAY

Depart from evil and do good; seek, inquire for,
and crave peace and pursue (go after) it!

PSALM 34:14 AMPC

Morning

SWALLOW THOSE WORDS.

Have a word on the tip of your tongue, a word you're dying to say but know will cause another person pain? *Eschew* it, and swallow it down! Ask God for help. He knows what's going on in your mind and in your listener's heart. He'll supply you with the right words.

Keep me from speaking and doing evil, Lord. I want peace!

Evening

PEACE IS LIKE CHOCOLATE!

Peace is more than words—it's action! Peace must be sought. It requires inquiry: "What can I do to make this situation better?" You must crave it like a decadent piece of chocolate, then go after it like you will never taste that kind of chocolate again! Vow tonight to make peace.

Precious Lord, I want to be a peacemaker,
not just in my words, but also in my actions. Guide me.

MEMORY VERSE OF THE DAY

*For I am convinced that neither death, nor life, nor angels,
nor principalities, nor things present, nor things to come, nor powers,
nor height, nor depth, nor any other created thing, will be able to
separate us from the love of God, which is in Christ Jesus our Lord.*

ROMANS 8:38–39 NASB

Morning

GOD WILL NEVER LEAVE ME.

Have you ever been separated from someone you loved? It's hard to be apart, isn't it? You go through a period of grieving, for sure, and wonder if you'll see each other again. This is only natural. What a blessed privilege to know that you'll never be separated from God. Dwell on that today.

*Father God, when I feel that pain of separation, remind me that
You are with me, loving me and comforting me.*

Evening

EVEN IF I MESS UP.

Have you ever lost a relationship because you messed up? Even if you mess up royally, God won't abandon you. Today's scripture memory verse is a promise that should bring you great peace. Read it. Learn it. Savor it! Nothing in the universe will cause God to leave you—ever.

*Thank You, God, for Your eternal promise of togetherness.
Ours is a relationship that will never be broken. What a comfort!*

MEMORY VERSE OF THE DAY

Casting all your anxiety on Him,
because He cares for you.

1 Peter 5:7 NASB

Morning ——————————————

I WILL CAST MY CARES ON HIM.

When you fish, you know how to cast your line into the water. It takes preparation, aim, and a sense of release. This is true when you cast your cares/anxieties on the Lord. It's a deliberate act: Make up your mind (prepare), place your worries at His feet (aim), and then let go (release)!

Lord, teach me to prepare, aim, and release my cares to You.
I need to let them go.

Evening ——————————————

HE CARRIES MY ANXIETY.

When you release your cares to God, He doesn't lose sleep over them like you do. He carries the weight as if it's nothing at all. So, the next time anxiety grips your heart, remember today's memory verse. God wants to carry your anxiety for you. Why? Because He loves you!

Dear heavenly Father, take my anxieties and worries.
Carry them for me. Release me from all my cares as I sleep tonight.

MEMORY VERSE OF THE DAY

*When I consider your heavens, the work of your fingers,
the moon and the stars, which you have set in place, what is mankind that
you are mindful of them, human beings that you care for them?*

PSALM 8:3–4 NIV

Morning

HE CARES FOR ME.

When you ponder God's creation—the heavens, the moon, and the stars—do
you feel tiny in comparison? You might be just a speck in the universe, but your
heavenly Father says you are more important to Him than the sun, moon, and
stars. He created you in His image, and He cares for you.

*Who am I, God, that You would think twice about me?
And yet You do. You love me, and for that I'm eternally grateful!*

Evening

I AM HIS GREATEST CREATION.

The next time you look up at the heavens, the next time you *ooh* and *aah* over a
majestic mountain or emerald waves crashing against the shoreline, remember
that those things, in all of their splendor, don't even come close to you, God's
greatest creation. Praise Him, tonight, for creating—you!

*Father, I don't often think of myself as Your greatest creation,
but I am! Thank You! I praise You for making me!*

MEMORY VERSE OF THE DAY

You've kept track of my every toss and turn through the sleepless nights,
each tear entered in your ledger, each ache written in your book.

PSALM 56:8 MSG

Morning

HE COUNTS MY TEARS.

You live in a fallen world. There are heartaches and disappointments. Some cause you to weep at times. God hates to see you cry, but remember this: He knows the big picture. Good things are coming your way. Until then, allow God to comfort you and dry your tears. He loves you.

Father, remind me that You are a God who sees my pain.
Comfort me in my times of sadness.

Evening

HE KNOWS WHEN I TOSS AND TURN.

Call out to God when you find yourself tossing and turning at night, or when tears drench your pillow. He is a God who sees, a God who knows. He is your Father, your daddy. Rest assured that He has not left you even for one moment. Imagine Him holding you tonight as you sleep.

In heaven there will be no more sadness. Tears will be a thing of the past.
But for now, dear Lord, just hold me.

MEMORY VERSE OF THE DAY

Lead a life worthy of your calling, for you have been called by God.
EPHESIANS 4:1 NLT

Morning

EVERYONE HAS A PURPOSE.

Everyone has a calling—a God-given purpose. To live a worthy life, you need to follow the path where God is leading you. Give this some thought today: Where do your talents lie? Do you feel God urging you to use them for Him? This might be your calling.

Lord, I want to live a worthy life for You!
How can I use the talents You gave me?

Evening

GOD WILL REVEAL MY CALLING.

Pray and ask God to reveal His calling for you. You might feel His answer in your heart, or the answer may come as you read the Bible. When you have an idea of your calling, go for it! Forget about obstacles. Ask God to guide you, and follow where He leads.

Father, where are You leading me?
What are You calling me to do? Show me, please.

MEMORY VERSE OF THE DAY

For the Spirit God gave us does not make us timid,
but gives us power, love and self-discipline.

2 TIMOTHY 1:7 NIV

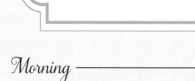

Morning

HE HELPS WHEN I FEEL AFRAID.

The Holy Spirit, also called The Helper, gives you all the resources you need to overcome fear. If you discipline your mind to trust Him, you will be unbeatable! Tap into His inexhaustible power whenever you need courage, and your banner of love for God will lift you above the fear of man.

Thank You, Heavenly Father, for the Holy Spirit, my helper.
Lead me to trust Him whenever I feel afraid.

Evening

POWER, LOVE, AND SELF–DISCIPLINE.

The Holy Spirit is not just a fear helper. He also provides power to overcome anxiety on the first day on a new job, self-discipline to say no to a calorie-loaded snack, the power to love unconditionally, and so many other things. You can rely on your Helper—always.

Holy Spirit, come and help me.
Lift me up. I can't do this alone.

MEMORY VERSE OF THE DAY

"Give, and it will be given to you. A good measure, pressed down, shaken together and running over, will be poured into your lap. For with the measure you use, it will be measured to you."

LUKE 6:38 NIV

Morning

GIVE. . .GIVE. . .GIVE!

Are you a giver or a taker? Want to overcome a "taker" attitude? Give more! That's right. Give even more. Giving turns focus from self toward others. Before long, you see the plight of the person you're helping, and it puts your selfish desires in perspective. Be a giver today.

Dear God, show me different ways to give.
Open my eyes to the needs of others.

Evening

TURN WANTING TO GIVING.

It's not wrong to want things unless those "things"—or the desire to have them—consume you. Today's memory verse speaks to your time of "wanting" because God promises to meet your needs when you give. If you find your "wants" consuming you, then you know what to do: Turn your thoughts toward giving—and give!

Lord, You already have my list of "wants," so I will stop thinking about them and turn my thoughts, instead, toward giving.

MEMORY VERSE OF THE DAY

As for God, his way is perfect: The LORD's word is flawless;
he shields all who take refuge in him.

PSALM 18:30 NIV

Morning ————————————————————

GOD IS MY SHIELD.

Marching bravely in front of the enemy without a proper shield would be foolish. It's equally foolish to think that you can battle the enemy of your soul without being properly equipped. When you trust the Lord, He shields you from evil. Let Him be your shield today. He's ready and waiting.

Almighty and Powerful God, be my shield.
Protect me from the enemy.

Evening ————————————————————

I NEED HIS HELP!

Do you often set out on your own saying, "I've got this. I don't need any help, thanks!" Don't say that to God! When you go it alone, you come out from under His safety net. Stick close to Him so He can be your refuge and shield. You need God's help!

Father God, I might think that I don't need Your help, but I do!
Help me to put aside my foolish thinking and ask for Your assistance.

MEMORY VERSE OF THE DAY

The Lord is good to those whose hope is in him, to the one who seeks him;
it is good to wait quietly for the salvation of the Lord.

LAMENTATIONS 3:25–26 NIV

Morning

HIS TIMETABLE, NOT MINE.

Patience is more than a virtue in today's wild and hypersonic world—it is an essential survival tool for a happy life. Scripture records that miracles unfold on God's timetable, not ours. How are you at waiting? Are you able to wait quietly and patiently for God to show up?

Dear Father, I'm not good at waiting patiently.
Help me learn to lean on You.

Evening

I WILL WAIT WITH PATIENCE.

God's hand is at work in your life when you are totally surrendered to His clock. He longs for His children to quit fretting and just wait patiently. So, tonight choose to give up your impatience and yield to God's calendar. The rewards will be great. His Word promises it.

Precious Lord, You are so patient with me!
Teach me to give up my impatience while I wait for You.

MEMORY VERSE OF THE DAY

And God said unto Moses, I AM THAT I AM: and he said, Thus shalt thou say unto the children of Israel, I AM hath sent me unto you.

ExODUS 3:14 KJV

Morning

GOD IS.

Are you plagued with regrets? Do you fret about the future? God doesn't. It isn't in His character to regret or fret. Although He existed in eternity past and will be in eternity future, God is neither past nor future. His most revered name is I AM. God is eternally *present*.

> *God, sometimes my thoughts slip to the past and the future.*
> *Help me, please, to live more in the present—with You!*

Evening

I AM BECAUSE HE IS!

God is. You are. Now, think about this: You are what you are, where you are, and how you are because God *is*. Be fully present with Him tonight. Keep your thoughts focused on right now. Ask God to show you who He wants You to be in this moment.

> *O, Father I've put aside all thoughts of the past and future.*
> *Show me who You want me to be in this very moment.*

MEMORY VERSE OF THE DAY

*Jesus said to Peter. . . "You don't care about the things of God,
but only about the things people think are important."*

MATTHEW 16:23 NCV

Morning —————————————————————

A GOD'S–EYE POINT OF VIEW.

Give this a try today. As you evaluate situations, people, and circumstances,
work to keep God's perspective in mind. Although you may not understand why
something is happening, be assured that He's got everyone's best interests at
heart. Try to see the world with a God's-eye point of view.

Jesus, help me to look at things through Your eyes.

Evening —————————————————————

ADJUST YOUR P.O.V.

In the Bible, we read that Jesus predicted that Peter would fly from His side when
the going got tough. (Matthew 26:75) Do you run and hide when challenges come
your way? Think about them with a God's-eye point of view, and His peace and
strength will empower you to face up to any conflict.

Father God, I need a P.O.V. readjustment.
Help me to align my thoughts with Yours.

MEMORY VERSE OF THE DAY

When [Peter] saw the strong wind and the waves,
he was terrified and began to sink. "Save me, LORD!" he shouted.

MATTHEW 14:30 NLT

Morning

FIX YOUR EYES ON HIM.

By faith, you climb out of the boat. You begin walking on the water and everything's fine. Then you take your eyes off Jesus, your faith falters. You feel the wind, see the waves. Panic sets in! Before you know it, you're sinking. Trust Jesus! He'll save you today. That's how He works.

Help me to get my eyes back on You, Jesus.

Evening

CALL JESUS.

What are you drowning in tonight? Work? Worries? An endless to-do list? Forget about that angry sea in front of you. Call Jesus. Reach out. Ask Him to take you by the hand and lead you to shore. He is your way to peace tonight and a good night's rest.

Jesus, come. Rescue me from my racing thoughts and busyness,
and lead me to rest.

MEMORY VERSE OF THE DAY

"Therefore, whoever takes the lowly position of this child is the greatest in the kingdom of heaven."

MATTHEW 18:4 NIV

Morning

GOD GETS THE GLORY.

Everything you are—everything you will ever be—is because of God's mercy and grace! Humility is pleasing to the Lord. He's not keen on hearing you brag about all your accomplishments. Sure, you've played a role in those things, but ultimately the glory goes to Him. Be sure to give Him credit.

Forgive me, Lord, when I forget that You are responsible for my successes. The glory goes to You. Thank You.

Evening

HUMBLE LIKE A CHILD.

Little children recognize that they are totally dependent on their caregivers. If only we would come to God with that same sort of attitude! God's love propels your growth and is at the core of all you do. It's time to stop taking credit. Tonight, acknowledge that He is the One responsible for it all.

Heavenly Father, everything I have— everything I've accomplished—is because of You.

MEMORY VERSE OF THE DAY

Give praise to the LORD, proclaim his name; make known among the nations what he has done. Sing to him, sing praise to him; tell of all his wonderful acts. Glory in his holy name; let the hearts of those who seek the LORD rejoice.

1 CHRONICLES 16:8–10 NIV

Morning

MY LIFE IS MY TESTIMONY.

Here's good news, straight from God's Word: When you live a praise-filled life, when you continually call on God's name, you can't help but let others know what He's doing in your life. You don't have to worry about "how" you tell them. Your very life—loaded with praise and thanksgiving—will be your testimony.

Lord, help me to always set a godly example for those around me. Allow them to see You through me.

Evening

PRAISE GOD!

When others observe how important the Lord is in your life and how centered you are in your faith, they will want what you have. So, don't be shy. Openly offer praise to God. Then watch as others take notice of your relationship with the King of kings.

Help me to be courageous, God, in sharing my faith with others. I want them to want You, too!

MEMORY VERSE OF THE DAY

"Then your Father,
who sees what is done in secret, will reward you."

MATTHEW 6:6 NIV

Morning

I LIVE TWO LIVES.

Think about this today: You live two lives. Your visible life is lived before others. Your secret life is lived solely before the Lord. Are they consistent? Sometimes the motives behind one's actions are to impress others. The real heart is revealed by what is done in secret, when only the Lord is watching.

God, help me walk consistently in Your truth.
May what I do in secret bring glory to You.

Evening

TREASURES IN HEAVEN.

Maybe you are weary of the world not noticing your good works. Never stop doing good works! They matter to God. He hears your prayers and sees what you do in secret to serve Him. Eternal treasures are being stored up for you in heaven. Your selfless acts will be rewarded.

Heavenly Father, when I get no recognition for doing good works,
I will remember that the only approval I need is Yours.

MEMORY VERSE OF THE DAY

"I will take away their stony, stubborn heart and give them a tender, responsive heart, so they will obey my decrees and regulations. Then they will truly be my people, and I will be their God."

EZEKIEL 11:19–20 NLT

Morning

DUTY VS. LOVE.

We try to obey God's rules. We pray, go to church, and give money to ministries. But how much of our obedience is out of a sense of duty? Meditate on this: God wants you to obey Him not because you're afraid He'll punish you if you don't, but because you love Him.

*Help me to love You more, God,
and to obey You because I love You.*

Evening

GOD CAN CHANGE MY HEART.

If you obey out of obligation, ask God to change your heart. Consider all He's done for you. Remind yourself that Jesus died for your sins freely, with no strings attached. When you meditate on His character and are convinced of His love for you, obedience won't be a duty but a delight.

Father, I praise You for the love that left heaven behind.

MEMORY VERSE OF THE DAY

"Everything is possible for one who believes." Immediately the boy's
father exclaimed, "I do believe; help me overcome my unbelief!"

MARK 9:23–24 NIV

Morning

WHO NEEDS A FAITH BOOSTER?

Everyone needs a faith booster, once in awhile. When your faith is waning you can cry out to God, and He'll give you the grace and power to erase your doubts and replace them with belief. Don't wait! Build up that belief! It leads to the successful working of miracles in your life.

Lord, I believe! Rid me of all doubt!

Evening

HIGHER GROUND.

When you are at your lowest, falling with no hope of rising back up, then you are most vulnerable to doubt. Remember: God will reach down and grab hold of you. He will pull you up and set you on higher ground. Ask Him to help your unbelief. Then expect His favor.

Lift me up on higher ground, Lord.
Help me rise above my unbelief.

DAY 234

MEMORY VERSE OF THE DAY

*But [the apostles] shook off the dust from their feet
against them and went to Iconium.*

ACTS 13:51 AMPC

Morning ————————————————————

SPIT IT OUT!

When a negative experience leaves a bad taste in your mouth, spit it out and move on. Don't let your mind linger on it or become obsessed with what should've happened. Just shake it off. New and better opportunities lie just around the corner. Trust the Lord to lead you.

> *Father, I am stuck thinking about that negative experience.
> Help me, please, to shake it off.*

Evening ————————————————————

MOVE ON.

Jesus told His disciples that if a town did not welcome them, they should leave and "shake off the dust from their feet." If you are in an unholy place or relationship, seek God in prayer and ask Him to help you move on—and when you do, leave the old behind. Shake the dust off your feet!

> *Help me move forward, Lord. Give me new direction!*

MEMORY VERSE OF THE DAY

Who satisfies your years with good things,
so that your youth is renewed like the eagle.

PSALM 103:5 NASB

Morning

HE MEETS MY EVERY NEED.

Young eagles go through many changes before reaching their full plumage. Through it all, God gives the eagle what it needs. The same is true with you, God's child. As you grow and develop in your faith, you go through changes. Some might seem difficult, but God knows what you need when you need it.

Father, from my youth through my old age, You provide for me.
You always know what I need.

Evening

GOOD THINGS ARE COMING.

You will go through seasons when you have to trust God more than usual. This is inevitable as you grow and develop. But God is faithful and will satisfy you with good things along the way. You can trust Him to meet your needs—just as He did when you were a child.

I trust You, Lord. Renew my faith. Make it fresh again.

MEMORY VERSE OF THE DAY

For he satisfies the thirsty and fills the hungry with good things.

PSALM 107:9 NIV

Morning

GOD GETS IT!

God won't leave you hungry and thirsty. When you come to Him—your spiritual "belly" empty—He fills you. How? With His love, peace, and joy; His provision. You won't walk away from your God-encounter saying things like, "I wish God understood all of the things I need/want." He gets it, and He cares.

*Almighty God, fill me up with Your love, peace, joy,
and provision. I'm hungry for You!*

Evening

FILL ME UP, LORD.

Maybe you're feeling empty. Meditate on today's memory verse. Then run to God. Lay it all out there. Tell Him about the aches, the loneliness, and the pain. He will sweep in and fill you up like you've never been filled before. You won't leave empty. That's His promise!

*Father, I feel so empty tonight. Hear my prayer.
Satisfy my hunger for a heart filled with joy.*

MEMORY VERSE OF THE DAY

*"This is how much God loved the world: He gave his Son, his one and
only Son. And this is why: so that no one need be destroyed;
by believing in him, anyone can have a whole and lasting life."*

JOHN 3:16 MSG

Morning

MEASURED IN SOULS.

God measures His wealth in souls, and that should be your focus, too. God loved
everyone—the world—so much that He sacrificed His own Son so people might live
forever in heaven. Be ready to share that idea with others. Someone needs to hear
it today! Watch for an opportunity to share.

*Which people in my life need to know You, Lord?
Lead me to them, so I can tell them about You.*

Evening

WE NEED EACH OTHER.

Try not to be so focused on your tasks that you miss the value of others. Learn
to focus on people, and really listen to what someone is saying. We need each
other—friends, family, or just passing acquaintances—in order to live successful
lives. And, of course, we all need Jesus!

*Dear God, I want to focus on others the way Jesus did.
Help me to listen and hear what's in their hearts.*

MEMORY VERSE OF THE DAY

*I would have lost heart, unless I had believed that I would see
the goodness of the LORD in the land of the living.*

PSALM 27:13 NKJV

Morning ———————————————————————

GOD'S ETERNAL GOODNESS.

God's goodness isn't just for when we get to heaven. He wants us to enjoy our lives here on earth. God cares about the things that you care about. Look for the good that He is doing in your life and find joy in knowing that your Friend deeply cares for you.

*Lord, thank You for being my Partner on my life's journey.
I'm grateful for all that You do for me—and for the joy I find in living.*

Evening ———————————————————————

I WILL LIVE JOYFULLY!

"The world isn't the way it used to be." We hear that a lot these days. In this world, it is easy to lose heart. But God gave you life to live it joyfully and abundantly! Instead of losing heart over bad news, make a real effort to make life joyful. Turn those negatives into something positive!

Every day, Father, I will seek good news. I will rejoice in it and share it with others.

MEMORY VERSE OF THE DAY

*The LORD will be your confidence and will
keep your foot from being caught.*

PROVERBS 3:26 ESV

Morning

CAREFUL. DON'T SLIP!

Ah, that moment when the conversation is going well, and then you let your words slip—and you find yourself caught in a relationship disaster. Learn from it. Before you speak, mentally run your words by God. You can trust Him to keep any relationship-ruining words from spilling out of your mouth.

*Dear God, stop me from speaking any relationship—
ruining words today—and every day!*

Evening

CONFIDENTIALLY, GOD. . .

If you are angry with someone or just plain don't like them, share it confidentially with God. Speak to others only those things that edify. Remember that God is listening. You'll be amazed at how good it feels not to get caught up in a tangle of destructive words.

*I want to build people up, Lord, instead of tearing them down.
I will speak as though only You are listening.*

MEMORY VERSE OF THE DAY

*"I am God and not a human.
I'm The Holy One and I'm here—in your very midst."*
HOSEA 11:9 MSG

Morning

HE IS HERE!

God is not human. He will not carry a grudge. He is not imperfect. He will not leave you. He is holy and He is right here—in your midst! Just reach out and touch Him. Talk to Him. Seek Him. Feel His presence. He is with you this morning, right now!

You are with me wherever I go, Lord! I praise Your name!

Evening

HE IS GOD.

Yes, God made humans in His image (Genesis 1:27), but that doesn't mean that humans are perfect like God. He is the almighty and Holy One, perfect in every way. God is everywhere, all the time, all knowing, and all powerful. Don't allow your relationship with Him to be so casual that you forget who He is.

O, Mighty God, I kneel before You tonight, praising You for your holiness and perfection. Thank You for loving me and making me Your child.

MEMORY VERSE OF THE DAY

Consult God's instruction and the testimony of warning.
If anyone does not speak according to this word,
they have no light of dawn.

ISAIAH 8:20 NIV

Morning —

I WILL RELY ON HIS WORD.

As you memorized the scriptures in this book, have you thought about them—*really* thought about them? Have you held them in your heart and called them out when you've needed them? Today's verse reminds you always to consult God's Word for instruction. Rely on *His* Word, not yours.

God, Your instructions are perfect,
and I know that I should always rely on them. Help me, please.

Evening —

WARNING! DANGER AHEAD.

Memorizing scripture, word for word is important. Why? Because there are false teachers in the world who twist God's Word and put their own spin on it. The words in the Bible are God-inspired words—straight from His mouth to your ears. Learn them so you can be warned of false teachings.

Precious Father, anyone who distorts Your words does not know You.
Lead me always to Your truth in the Bible.

MEMORY VERSE OF THE DAY

Yes, my soul, find rest in God; my hope comes from him.
Truly he is my rock and my salvation; he is my fortress,
I will not be shaken.

PSALM 62:5–6 NIV

Morning

I WILL NOT BE SHAKEN.

Grab hold of the promise in today's verse. Truly believe that life's shakings won't affect you from the inside out. God is your rock. That means He's the safest thing to grab onto. He's your fortress and when you take hold of His hand, you won't be shaken. What an amazing promise!

Father, You are my rock and my salvation,
my fortress in times of trouble. Protect me. Hold my hand.

Evening

I WILL REST IN HIM.

Finding rest in God is like being asleep in your comfortable bed while a wicked storm rages outside. You are oblivious to the trees bending to the rampant wind and the rain beating the pavement. Inside, you rest secure, trusting in the safety of your Fortress, Your God. Find rest in Him tonight.

O, God, bless me with a restful night's sleep. With You nearby,
nothing can hurt me. I sleep safe and secure in Your love.

MEMORY VERSE OF THE DAY

*So you must change your hearts and lives! Come back to God,
and he will forgive your sins. Then the Lord will send the time of rest.*

Acts 3:19 NCV

Morning

U–TURN!

We all have moments when we realize we've been traveling in the wrong direction. Then we come face to face with God—through the person of His Son, Jesus,—and do a quick 180-degree turnaround. When we make that turn and repent, He forgives us. Repent today. Ask God to help you go the right way.

*Lord, sometimes I mess up and let sin get the best of me. I'm sorry.
I realize that I've made a mistake. Forgive me and set me
back on the right path.*

Evening

A SEASON OF REST.

You know when sin has a hold on you. Your soul is uneasy, and so is your mind. Negative thoughts saturate your thinking. You long for peace. When you let go of sin and repent, things change. Suddenly, you heart and mind turn toward God, and He gives you a season of rest.

*Father, my soul and my mind are at peace, thanks to Your forgiveness.
Now I can rest!*

MEMORY VERSE OF THE DAY

I will sing to the LORD, because he is good to me.

PSALM 13:6 NLT

Morning

A FOUR–IN–ONE WORKOUT.

Sing to the Lord this morning! Singing is good for you in so many ways. Physically, it exercises your lungs and heart. Emotionally, it lifts your spirits. It also benefits you mentally and spiritually. So, don't be shy about singing a praise song. Belt out a tune. Give yourself a four-in-one workout!

Father, I will sing praises to You because You have been so good to me.

Evening

BUT I CAN'T SING!

If you can't carry a tune, God doesn't care. Your singing is sweet to His ears and reaps benefits galore! But, if you refuse to sing, then spend some time reading the book of Psalms. It overflows with words of praise. Read them out loud to the Lord. He loves hearing your voice.

I'm sorry, God, for being shy about singing, but please accept these words of praise. They come from my heart.

MEMORY VERSE OF THE DAY

*"Lord, there is no one besides You to help in the battle
between the powerful and those who have no strength."*

2 Chronicles 14:11 nasb

Morning

I CAN COUNT ON HIM.

Nothing is certain in life. Things can change in an instant. God is the one sure thing you can count on. Riches, people, and possessions may fail you, but God never will. Face life with assurance that when you are weak, He is your strength. He won't let you down. That's His promise.

*Lord, You, and You alone, are the only One I can always count on.
Great is Your faithfulness!*

Evening

FIGHT FOR ME, LORD!

Find a quiet place in your house tonight where you can pray uninterrupted. Sit there quietly. Focus on seeking the Lord. One by one, put your battles in His hands. Trust Him to take each one and fight it for you. Remember, He is your strength. You can count on him to fight, and win!

Thank You, God, for taking my battles into Your hands!

MEMORY VERSE OF THE DAY

For we are labourers together with God:
ye are God's husbandry, ye are God's building.

1 CORINTHIANS 3:9 KJV

Morning

I WORK FOR THE LORD.

God allows you to work with Him to accomplish great things for His kingdom. He could have chosen angels or another method to fulfill His work that would have required less dealing with stubbornness and excuses; but God chose to use you—His human creation. Work well for Him today.

O, great God, it is an honor to serve You.
Help me to remember it is You whom I work for.

Evening

FATHER, WORK IN MY LIFE.

Not only did God choose to use you in His work, He also continues to work in your life to mold you into the masterpiece He has planned. The more you allow Him to do in you, the more He will be able to do *through* you. How has God changed you, so far?

Father, I ask You to work in my life that I might be useful to Your work.

MEMORY VERSE OF THE DAY

*"Why do you look at the speck of sawdust in your brother's eye
and pay no attention to the plank in your own eye?"*

LUKE 6:41 NIV

Morning

DON'T JUDGE!

Think about this today: God tells us not to judge others. After all, He doesn't look at your outward appearance. He doesn't worry about your political affiliation or anything else in your life that is open to interpretation. He looks at the heart and judges by whether you have a personal relationship with Him.

God, please forgive me for the times that I have judged others.

Evening

GRANT ME A GENTLE SPIRIT.

Jesus reminds you through His sawdust/plank analogy that none of us are blameless. It's important to put your own shortcomings into perspective when you face the temptation to judge others. Make it your every mission to work on removing the plank from your eye and praising God for His gift of grace!

*Help me, Father, to develop a gentle spirit that can share Your love
and hope in a nonjudgmental way.*

MEMORY VERSE OF THE DAY

For sin shall no longer be your master,
because you are not under the law, but under grace.

ROMANS 6:14 NIV

 Morning ──────────────────

TRAPPED.

Sin traps you in a life you don't want. You wish for better things—freedom, peace, tranquility—but they seem elusive at best. The only "master" in your life should be the One you've submitted your heart to—Jesus! His grace and mercy are a lovely substitute for the sins of the past.

Jesus, be my safety net today.
Keep me from getting trapped by sin.

Evening ──────────────────────

GOOD NEWS!

There's good news from the Word of God! When you come to Christ, when you accept His gift of salvation, you are no longer in chains (or bondage) to sin. Those shackles are broken the moment you give your heart to the Lord. Praise Him tonight for His gift of salvation!

O, Jesus, where would I be without You?
Thank You, so much, for Your gift of salvation!

MEMORY VERSE OF THE DAY

*No temptation has overtaken you except such as is common to man;
but God is faithful, who will not allow you to be tempted beyond
what you are able, but with the temptation will also make
the way of escape, that you may be able to bear it.*

1 Corinthians 10:13 NKJV

Morning

MORE THAN I CAN BEAR.

Do you feel like your burden is too heavy to bear? If so, today's memory verse should bring great comfort. God won't allow you to be tempted beyond what you can bear. Instead, He always provides a way out. He longs to see you walk in total freedom, above the temptations of this life.

*Father, please, enough! I'm so done with this.
Please provide me with a way out.*

Evening

ESCAPE!

Ask God for an escape route tonight. Freedom is yours, but you must take action—trust in God's faithfulness and be prepared to make your escape! Don't allow depression and anxiety to lock your knees. Stay flexible, and be willing to run toward the light when the moment comes.

*Lord, show me the way out of this mess. I trust in Your faithfulness,
so take this situation, and turn it around for good.*

MEMORY VERSE OF THE DAY

Jesus Christ is the same yesterday and today and forever.
HEBREWS 13:8 NIV

Morning ——————————————————————

JESUS DOESN'T CHANGE.

Rest assured today that Jesus remains the same—yesterday, today, and forever. Minute by minute, you can look to Him for guidance, reassurance, and peace of mind. You can rest in the fact that Jesus, your Rock, is always there, waiting to strengthen you and meet your every need. Trust Him!

Thank You, Jesus, for being my Rock, my Refuge, and my Rest.

Evening ——————————————————————

JESUS IS—ALWAYS!

No matter how bleak the world looks, no matter what crisis you are going through, you don't have to worry, for although heaven and earth may pass away, God's words—the anchor of your spirit, the bread of your life, that which gives you peace beyond understanding—will remain forever. Rest on that thought tonight.

Ah, Lord, what a relief to know that in this ever-changing world,
You are always there, waiting for me to come to You, loving me and sheltering me.

MEMORY VERSE OF THE DAY

For all have sinned, and come short of the glory of God.
ROMANS 3:23 KJV

Morning

CONFESS, RECEIVE, MOVE ON.

Sin is not a politically correct topic these days. Yet God talks about sin all throughout His Word. Satan loves to remind us of our sins to make us feel guilty. But God never intended for us to do that. Instead, God wants us to confess our sins, receive His forgiveness, and move on.

Lord, make me ever aware of Your grace and forgiveness,
so that I may move on without guilt.

Evening

EVERYONE SINS.

What sins have separated you from God today? Draw near the throne of grace tonight and receive His pardon. He longs for you to come near to Him, and He will cover you with Jesus' robe of righteousness, so that you don't have to feel guilt or shame anymore.

Father God, forgive me for the sins I've committed today.
Remove my guilt and shame, and allow my soul to rest.

MEMORY VERSE OF THE DAY

Taking the five loaves and the two fish and looking up to heaven,
[Jesus] gave thanks.

MARK 6:41 NIV

Morning ───────────────────────

IT'S ABOUT WHAT I HAVE!

Jesus' disciples saw what they didn't have. But you know better! Look at what you do have and give it to Jesus. He'll bless, and then multiply it! And in the end, you'll not only be satisfied but also find you have more than enough! You'll go from lack to plenty!

Jesus, I bring what I have and give it to You.
Do with it what You will!

Evening ───────────────────────

I WILL ACT ON GOD'S WORD.

God wants you to put the lessons in His Word into action. Tonight, make a plan to act on today's memory verse. Bake, or buy, two loaves of your favorite bread. Keep one for yourself and prayerfully consider who God wants to have the extra loaf. After giving it to that person, watch God's love multiply!

Almighty God, who should receive my gift of bread?
I long to see Your love shine on someone who needs it.

MEMORY VERSE OF THE DAY

He fixed his attention on them,
expecting to receive something from them.

ACTS 3:5 ESV

Morning

I WILL EXPECT GOD'S BLESSINGS.

Remember that faith and expectation go hand in hand. When you pray, firmly believing you will be receiving what you've asked for, miraculous things happen. Today, make an effort to fix your attention on the God of all creation, the Doer of the impossible, and expect to be blessed!

Lord, praying in Your name releases power! I believe I'll receive!

Evening

HIS BLESSINGS SURROUND ME.

Fixing your attention on God means keeping your eyes open for His blessings. They might be small and elusive, there for you to grab onto. Or they may be big and bold, and impossible to miss. Today's verse reminds you to expect God's blessings. Look! They are all around you!

I will fix my attention on You, God, and anticipate Your blessings.

MEMORY VERSE OF THE DAY

This is the confidence we have in approaching God: that if we ask anything according to his will, he hears us. And if we know that he hears us—whatever we ask—we know that we have what we asked of him.

1 JOHN 5:14–15 NIV

Morning —————————————————————

GOD HEARS ME.

Isn't it wonderful to know that God's hearing is impeccable? Not only does He hear your cries, He tunes in to your whispers. He even hears the silent cries of the heart—the ones you don't vocalize. Today, His ear is ever inclined toward you, waiting for your next breath, your next word.

Dear God, listen to my heart and my whispered prayers today.
Give me what I need.

Evening —————————————————————

LOUD AND CLEAR.

Think about it. God has billions of other people to listen to, but still, He has time for your thoughts, your ideas, and your concerns. He hears you and He cares. What an amazing promise! When you pray tonight, be assured that your heavenly Father listens. He hears you, loud and clear!

Father, how amazing that You hear my voice above all others!
Hear my prayer tonight, O Lord!

MEMORY VERSE OF THE DAY

He forgives all my sins. He heals all my sicknesses.

PSALM 103:3 NIrV

Morning

GOD STILL HEALS.

Along with forgiveness of sin, the Lord's goal is for us to live at peace in this life. Sometimes we forget that we can ask Him to heal our bodies, our minds, and our hearts. Remember: God is still in the healing business. He longs to see us walk in wholeness. Believe it!

Lord, pain and suffering is all around, still, I believe that You love us and heal our bodies, minds, and hearts.

Evening

IN HIS TIME.

We don't always understand how God's healing works—why some receive remarkable healings and others aren't healed until they get to heaven. But we are told to ask. So, perhaps tonight is your time. Are you sick? Hurting? Ask the Lord to heal, and then trust Him with the timing.

Heal me, O, Lord! Bring healing comfort to all who are sick and hurting tonight.

MEMORY VERSE OF THE DAY

*"Bless my family; keep your eye on them always.
You've already as much as said that you would, Master GOD!
Oh, may your blessing be on my family permanently!"*

2 SAMUEL 7:29 MSG

Morning ————————————————————————

HE WILL BLESS MY FAMILY.

Today, recommit yourself to trusting God with your family. Don't fret and don't try to fix people. That's not your job, after all. And besides, God's keeping an eye on everyone. He's said it, and you can believe it. It's in His master plan to bless your family. . .permanently!

> *God, I confess I sometimes struggle where my family is concerned.
> I want to fix people. Remind me—that's Your job!*

Evening ————————————————————————

I TRUST HIM WITH MY FAMILY.

Did you know that you can trust God with both your own life and the lives of your family members? You can trust Him with their dreams, their goals, their aspirations, their attitudes, their reactions, their problems. You can trust Him to handle any relationship problems. God's got it covered. All of it.

> *Father God, I entrust my entire family to You.
> Draw them near to You, bless them, heal their hurts, and guide them.*

MEMORY VERSE OF THE DAY

By his divine power, God has given us everything
we need for living a godly life.

2 PETER 1:3 NLT

Morning

JUST SAY NO.

Stress makes you feel like a grape in a winepress, but there's good news. God has given you everything you need—but you must choose to use the wisdom He's provided. Don't be afraid to say no when stress says you can't add one more thing to your to-do list. Limit your commitments today.

Lord, help me to do what I can do;
and I'll trust You to do for me those things that I can't do.

Evening

EASE THE PRESSURE.

Somehow, you kept pushing forward, not always sure where the strength came from, but thankful, in the end, that you made it through the day. Talk with God and ask Him to help you to ease the pressure where you can. Then know that His power will do the rest.

I keep pushing myself, God, and I know that You don't want me to.
Help me to prioritize the most important tasks and to say no to the rest.

MEMORY VERSE OF THE DAY

The Lord will work out his plans for my life—
for your faithful love, O Lord, endures forever.

PSALM 138:8 NLT

Morning

GOD IS ON MY SIDE.

Today's memory verse is a reminder of God's faithful, forever love. When all seems lost, when goals seem unattainable, when you feel unloved, don't despair! God is working things out. After all, He loves you. So take heart! You've got the Supreme Being on your side today—and forever!

Take my hand today, dear Lord. Walk by my side,
and allow me to feel Your enduring love.

Evening

FOREVER LOVE.

Remember tonight that God loves you. Maybe you don't see His plans working out in your life, but be assured that God is working His plan. Be patient and remain faithful. Trust in His faithfulness to you. Ask Him to reassure you of His love. Then open your heart to receive it.

Sometimes, I forget, Father, just how much You love me.
Reassure me of Your love. Keep working out Your plans for me.

MEMORY VERSE OF THE DAY

"I leave you peace; my peace I give you. I do not give it to you as the world does. So don't let your hearts be troubled or afraid."

JOHN 14:27 NCV

Morning

PEACE LIKE NO OTHER.

Memorize today's verse and repeat it to yourself, again and again. No wonder the angels were excited when Jesus was born. He came to give humankind peace like no other. All you have to do to obtain His peace is commune with God. With that peace upon you, fret and fear disappear!

Today, Lord, I will concentrate on the peace You give me in all situations.

Evening

PEACE RAINS.

Close your eyes and imagine the peace of Jesus raining upon you. His is a gentle rain, one that refreshes you. It is a cleansing rain that washes away your sin. Allow His peace to flow like a river through you. Let it carry you away to a restful night's sleep.

Jesus, let Your peace rain upon me.
Allow it to fill me up and take me away from all the stress.

MEMORY VERSE OF THE DAY

"This Book of the Law shall not depart from your mouth, but you shall meditate on it day and night, so that you may be careful to do according to all that is written in it. For then you will make your way prosperous, and then you will have good success."

JOSHUA 1:8 ESV

Morning ───────────────────────

THE SECRET TO SUCCESS.

Do you want to be successful? Then meditate on scripture and put it into action every day. Especially concentrate on God's rules and promises. Today's verse reminds you to be careful to *do* according to what is written in God's Word. Allow His scripture to guide you toward success today.

Dear God, help me to do according to Your instructions, being careful not to add to them with my own thoughts and words.

Evening ───────────────────────

MEDITATE DAY AND NIGHT.

After you memorize your daily scripture, what do you do with it? Do you act on it throughout the day? Get into the habit of memorizing scripture first thing in the morning. Put it into action during the day, and then meditate on the scripture before you say your nightly prayers.

Father, reveal Yourself to me through today's memory verse. Teach me. Show me the way to prosperity and success.

MEMORY VERSE OF THE DAY

Jesus replied, "Very truly I tell you, no one can see the kingdom of God unless they are born again."

JOHN 3:3 NIV

Morning

HOW TO BE BORN AGAIN.

Being born again is one of the simplest—but most profound—moves you can make. When you acknowledge your need for Christ, humble yourself, and cry out for forgiveness for your past sins, He grants not only mercy and grace, but a whole new life. A complete and total fresh start!

*Father God, I need Jesus. Forgive me for my sins,
and grant me a fresh, new life.*

Evening

MY KEY TO GOD'S KINGDOM.

Born again. What do you think of when you read those words? Born again: Your spirit is awakened from slumber, stepping into a brand-new existence, one that will last from now until eternity. Brand-new. Old things passed away. Born again! Your key to God's kingdom. What an amazing and wonderful gift!

*Thank You, Almighty God, for the gift of being born again.
Old things passed away. All things are new!*

MEMORY VERSE OF THE DAY

"Be strong and courageous. Do not be afraid or terrified because
of them, for the LORD your God goes with you;
he will never leave you nor forsake you."

DEUTERONOMY 31:6 NIV

Morning ———————————————————

I HATE TESTS!

Have you ever failed a test? You're not expected to sail through every one. That's why they're called tests! There is only One who has never failed a test, and He's proven Himself faithful in every area. Jesus won't fail you. In fact, He can't fail because He's perfect. Think about that today.

Jesus, tests make me anxious, but I know that You will give me strength
and courage to get through them. You've got this!

Evening ———————————————————

GOD NEVER FAILS.

"God won't fail me." Repeat those words several times in a row. They're true, you know. Today's memory verse is comforting, especially when you're facing a trial. You might not pass the test, but Jesus will. He always will! So, count on Him to make things right. Just trust Him.

O, God, You won't ever fail me! What a wonderful promise
to hang onto. Thank You!

MEMORY VERSE OF THE DAY

They are not of the world, even as I am not of the world.

JOHN 17:16 NASB

Morning

WORLDLY MESSAGES.

The world sends messages about how we should look and act. But believers in Christ are not of this world. We are in it, but not of it. We are visitors here, and heaven will be our eternal home. Today, do your best to avoid believing the things the world whispers to you.

Father, remind me today to tune out the world as I tune
in to what You have to say to me.

Evening

MY HEART DEFINES ME.

It's okay if you're not perfect in the world's eyes. God sees you as His beautiful child, important enough to give His Son's life for! It is the heart that defines you, and if your heart is turned toward Jesus, instead of the world, then your outer beauty will shine brighter than any diamond.

Dear God, I don't care what the world thinks of me,
but I do care that You love me and live in my heart.

MEMORY VERSE OF THE DAY

*The Spirit and the bride say, "Come!" And let the one who hears say,
"Come!" Let the one who is thirsty come; and let the one
who wishes take the free gift of the water of life.*

REVELATION 22:17 NIV

Morning

JESUS—THE BEST GIFT.

Jesus gave His earthly life away without our asking Him to or paying Him. Love led Him to give all He could to draw some to Himself. He knew many would deny His gift, still Jesus offered Himself freely. Do you know someone who needs the best free gift in the world? Tell them about Jesus!

*Jesus, I accept Your gift! Thank You for giving away
Your earthly life so I can have eternal life.*

Evening

FREE—NO STRINGS ATTACHED!

Meditate on today's memory verse. As we drink deeply of the water of life, we recognize God's great gift. Grateful, we seek out ways to serve Him. But even if we gave all we had, we could never repay God. His gift would still be free—no strings attached.

*O, Jesus, there is nothing I can do to repay You for Your great gift,
and You expect nothing in return. I love You, Jesus! I love You!*

MEMORY VERSE OF THE DAY

The Lord is a place of safety for those who have been treated badly.
He keeps them safe in times of trouble.

PSALM 9:9 NIrV

Morning

LORD, LIFT ME UP.

Today's news media seems to bear nothing but bad reports. It's enough to beat anyone down—unless they make a concerted effort to turn their thoughts, heart, and soul toward God. Will you do that today? With Him, you are safe. Let the Lord lift you above the world's chaos.

Dear Lord, when the world's news gets me down,
I know that You will lift me up.

Evening

I WILL HOLD ONTO THE GOOD NEWS.

Avoid watching the late news broadcast tonight. Instead, go to bed a little early and spend that time with Jesus. A break from the headlines may be just the thing to lift your soul, recharge your spirit, and change your outlook. And before you sleep, read from God's Word—it holds only good news!

Keep me safe from the world, O, Lord.
Help me to hold on to the Good News in Your Word.

MEMORY VERSE OF THE DAY

"You will seek me and find me,
when you seek me with all your heart."

Jeremiah 29:13 esv

Morning

GOD IS ALWAYS WITH ME.

Did you wake up feeling far from God? It's not He who has moved; you have. He is never more than a heartbeat away. When you come near to Him, whole heart in hand, He will be near to you. Concentrate on Him all day today. Ask Him to fill you up with His presence.

Almighty Father, forgive me for pulling away from You.
Fill me up with Your presence today.

Evening

I WILL SEEK HIM WHOLE–HEARTEDLY.

It's easy to pull away from God without knowing it. Worldly chaos gets in the way—and Satan loves that. When you feel overwhelmed by tasks and worries, stop and seek God. Seek Him as often as you have to every day. You will find Him when you seek Him, not halfheartedly, but with your whole heart.

God, Help me to keep the world from getting in the way.
I will seek You every day with my whole heart.

MEMORY VERSE OF THE DAY

. . .to the praise of his glorious grace,
which he has freely given us in the One he loves.

EPHESIANS 1:6 NIV

Morning

GOD'S UNMERITED FAVOR.

When you love someone, you want to bless them. The same is true with God. He loves you so much that He wants to freely bestow His love, His grace, and His mercy on you, even when you don't deserve it. That's why it's called "grace," after all—it's God's unmerited favor.

O, Lord, I praise you for the grace that comes through Your Son, Jesus.
Your love overwhelms me!

Evening

AMAZING GRACE.

Here's the best news of all: the Lord freely gives. That means He's not standing with hand outstretched, waiting for you to somehow pay Him back. His grace is a free gift, though it cost His Son dearly. So, you can't take advantage of this amazing grace. You must treasure it as the gift it is.

Father God, I treasure Your amazing gift of grace.
Help me never to take it for granted.

MEMORY VERSE OF THE DAY

*"For the LORD your God is a compassionate God; He will not
fail you nor destroy you nor forget the covenant with
your fathers which He swore to them."*

DEUTERONOMY 4:31 NASB

Morning

I PLEDGE. . .

Think about the word "covenant" in today's verse. What does it mean? A covenant is a binding agreement, a pledge. Think today about the covenant you have made with God. What have you pledged to Him? If you haven't kept your pledge, remember His compassion. If you ask, He will forgive you.

*Dear God, forgive me for not keeping my promises,
those things I have pledged to You. I will try to do better.*

Evening

GOD'S COVENANT WITH ME.

God enters into a covenant with you. He agrees to stick with you, no matter what. What do you agree to? To walk with Jesus all the days of your life. This agreement is an understanding between God and you: you're linked. Bonded. Held together through the work of Jesus on the cross.

*Father, I pledge to walk with Jesus my whole life.
Thank You for Your Son, and thank You
for sticking with me, no matter what.*

MEMORY VERSE OF THE DAY

The king's heart is a stream of water in the hand of the LORD;
he turns it wherever he will.

PROVERBS 21:1 ESV

Morning

WHEN RELATIONSHIPS GET TOUGH.

Relationships can be difficult. Even when communication is good and both people are Christians, there is still conflict when two human beings have a long-term relationship. How do we get beyond competing desires that conflict with each other and harm our relationships? By putting them into "the hand of the Lord!"

Father, my relationship with _____ is not what it should be.
Take us into Your hands and help us.

Evening

PRAYER IS THE KEY.

You can pray for your own heart to change as well as those you're in conflict with. God can shape your affections, and He can change the minds of those for whom you pray. It is not difficult for Him, yet it's easy to forget to ask. What relationships in your life need prayer tonight?

Hear my prayers tonight, O, Lord. Please bring Your love
and healing touch into my relationships.

MEMORY VERSE OF THE DAY

God, are you avoiding me?
Where are you when I need you?
PSALM 10:1 MSG

Morning ───────────────────

MISSING IN ACTION.

If you're in a season where God seems to be missing in action, take time to listen more attentively. If you still can't hear His voice, remember there are times when He chooses to remain silent. Perhaps He's just waiting to see if you're going to act on what He's already taught you.

God, why are You so quiet lately?
Are You waiting for me to do something?

Evening ───────────────────

THINK. THEN ACT!

God is not in the avoiding business. If His voice isn't clear right now, think back to the last thing you heard Him speak to your heart. Act on that thing. Just keep walking in consistent faith, love, and hope. And before long, you'll be hearing His voice again. . .crystal clear.

Father God, speak to me. Tell me again what I need to hear,
and then I will act on it. I'm waiting to hear Your voice.

MEMORY VERSE OF THE DAY

*"When my life was fainting away, I remembered the Lord,
and my prayer came to you, into your holy temple."*

JONAH 2:7 ESV

Morning

I WILL REMEMBER THE LORD.

Think about today's memory verse. What image do those words "fainting away" call up in your mind? Fainting away—the light turns to darkness, and you slip into unconsciousness. This is what happens when you forget the Lord. Remember Him, all the time, every day, so your life won't slip away.

Father, I will remember and call on You, morning, noon, at night—always!

Evening

HE WILL RESCUE ME.

Sometimes people do not seek God until they are in a deep pit of despair. But the wonderful thing is that God will listen to your prayer no matter how far you've fallen. Don't wait! Pray to God tonight. He'll rescue you and forgive you because you are precious in His sight.

Lord, lift me up into Your arms! Rescue me from my fainting spell.

MEMORY VERSE OF THE DAY

*"Only fear the LORD and serve him faithfully with all your heart.
For consider what great things he has done for you."*

1 SAMUEL 12:24 ESV

 Morning ———————————————————————

MIRACLES, BIG AND SMALL.

Today's verse tells you to consider the great things that God has done for you. He has filled your life with miracles, big and small. The first of those miracles is you! He made you and gave you life. Spend today meditating on what else God has done for you.

*O, Lord, I could never thank You enough for all you have done
for me, but I will serve You—faithfully.*

Evening ———————————————————————

I LOVE YOU, GOD!

The Bible contains myriad accounts of the magnificent things God has done for His people. But He didn't stop there. Today, you discovered that God has done many amazing things in your own life. And will continue to do so! What a wonderful God He is. Love Him with all your heart.

*My heart belongs to You, Father God.
Thank You for working in my life. I love You!*

MEMORY VERSE OF THE DAY

Guard my words as your most precious possession.
Write them down, and also keep them deep within your heart.

PROVERBS 7:2–3 TLB

Morning

GUARD HIS WORDS.

How important for you are the daily memory verses? Today's verse tells you to guard them as your most precious possession. Why? Because they help you resist temptation, make wise decisions, and discern God's will for you. They strengthen and comfort you. Memorize them. Then hold them close so they're ready when you need them.

Heavenly Father, I will memorize Your words and guard them in my heart.

Evening

WRITE THEM DOWN.

Today's verse also tells you to write out your scripture verses. Writing them is one good way to memorize them. But you can also keep a scripture journal in which you write down your thoughts about a specific verse—this is another way that God might speak to you. Give it a try.

Dear God, as I write and meditate on scripture, speak to my heart.
Give me a deeper understanding of You.

MEMORY VERSE OF THE DAY

In peace I will lie down and sleep,
for you alone, Lord, make me dwell in safety.

PSALM 4:8 NIV

Morning

AH, SLEEP. . .

How well did you sleep last night? Were you so busy juggling job, family, meals, dishes, laundry, that you were wound up like a clock by the time you finally tumbled into bed? Keep your mind on God today. Slow down, and tonight He will bless you with sleep.

I will keep my mind on You today, Lord.
Remind me to slow down and not let stress get to me.

Evening

I DWELL IN GOD'S SAFETY.

Here's a wonderful scriptural promise: When you "dwell" in God's safety (resting in the security that He's got things handled), you can lie down and sleep in peace. No troubling thoughts. No tossing and turning. Just sweet, joyous sleep! God's got all your cares and worries safe in His hands. So—sleep!

Father, I will lie down and sleep in peace,
for You alone make me dwell in safety.

MEMORY VERSE OF THE DAY

When I awake, I will be satisfied with seeing your likeness.

PSALM 17:15 NIV

Morning

JESUS IS THERE.

Picture a boxer knocked out in the ring. Everything is fuzzy. Then, breaking through the fog and haze, he clamps eyes on the Lord. Not his opponent. Not the crowd, but Jesus. Wow! That's like what we go through when we've been badly hurt. Jesus is there for us! Remember that today.

*Jesus, when I've been hurt, I will remember that You are there for me.
You are always there for me!*

Evening

WHEN I CAN'T SEE STRAIGHT. . .

When nothing makes sense, when you can't see straight, one Person is in your line of sight: Jesus. When you focus on Him, you don't have to be afraid. You also don't have to come up with a strategy for solving your problem. All you have to do is look into Jesus' eyes and trust that He's got this.

*When everything looks fuzzy, You are the one who brings clarity.
Seeing You standing before me is all that I need, Father.*

MEMORY VERSE OF THE DAY

Whom have I in heaven but you? And earth has nothing I desire besides you. My flesh and my heart may fail, but God is the strength of my heart and my portion forever.

PSALM 73:25–26 NIV

Morning ———————————————————

GOD'S STRENGTH SHINES THROUGH.

In your weakness, God's strength shines through. His strength surpasses yours, even on your best day. It's the same strength that spoke the heavens and the earth into existence, parted the Red Sea, and it's the same strength that made the journey up the hill to the cross. God is your strength today.

Lord, invigorate me all day with Your strength.

Evening ———————————————————

TAP INTO HIS STRENGTH.

So how do you tap into God's strength? There's really only one way. Come into His presence. Spend some quiet time with Him tonight. Acknowledge your weakness, then allow His strong arms to encompass you. There's really nothing else in heaven or on earth to compare. God is all you will ever need.

Father, I feel so weak at times. It's hard just to put one foot in front of the other. But I know You are my strength.

MEMORY VERSE OF THE DAY

Do not be wise in your own eyes; fear the LORD and shun evil.
This will bring health to your body and nourishment to your bones.
PROVERBS 3:7–8 NIV

Morning ————————————————————

NOURISH ME, LORD!

Feeling run down? Has your spiritual fervor left? Obeying and living by God's principles produces life and health. Just as you exercise to strengthen your body, you must use your spiritual muscles to attain the strength, peace, and prosperity you need and desire. Ask God to nourish you today.

Dear Lord, please help me out of my spiritual and physical rut.
Nourish me today.

Evening ————————————————————

SPIRITUAL STAMINA.

As you pray, read, and meditate on God's Word, you increase your spiritual stamina. Although your circumstances may not change, the Lord gives you a new perspective filled with the hope and assurance that you may have lacked before. Exercising your faith produces character and a stronger foundation of trust in the Lord.

As I seek Your strength, God, revive my soul and
touch my body with Your healing power.

MEMORY VERSE OF THE DAY

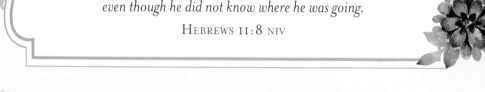

*By faith Abraham, when called to go to a place he would
later receive as his inheritance, obeyed and went,
even though he did not know where he was going.*

HEBREWS 11:8 NIV

Morning

WHAT IS REAL FAITH?

Real faith is stepping out into the unknown, willing to go where God has called you even though you don't know where you're headed. The great thing about it is that when absolute faith moves people, God moves mountains. Do you feel God urging you to step out in faith today?

*Father, help me to walk in absolute faith.
I'm ready to go where You lead me.*

Evening

TAKE THAT FIRST STEP.

Stepping out in faith is only the first step in your journey. With each additional step, you must trust the Lord. It might take a long time to reach the destination He has planned for you. But be assured, good things await you there. Don't stop! Keep walking in faith, knowing that God is with you.

*Almighty God, if I become afraid on this journey and want to stop,
remind me that You are leading me. Let's go!*

MEMORY VERSE OF THE DAY

"Neither fear them nor fear their words. . .
neither fear their words nor be dismayed at their presence."

 EZEKIEL 2:6 NASB

Morning ────────────────────────

OH, THOSE BULLIES!

We all have to deal with difficult people; those who make us bristle in their presence or who say things that wound our spirits. Fortunately, you have God's protection. When you abide in Christ's love, you need not fear the bullies. Be brave. Be bold. Believe. And all will be well.

Father, when someone lords over me or acts like a bully,
I won't be afraid—because Your love protects me.

Evening ────────────────────────

PRAY FOR A CHANGE OF HEART.

Tonight, begin praying for someone who is difficult to be around or has wounded you with his or her words. Pray for that person every day until you feel the peace of God transform your heart from bitter to benevolent. That's amazing grace! Ask God to change their heart, too.

Lord Jesus, help me find the words to pray for _____.
Soften my heart toward him/her, and soften his/her heart, too.

MEMORY VERSE OF THE DAY

Jesus replied, "What is impossible with man is possible with God."
LUKE 18:27 NIV

Morning

INSIDE INTELLIGENCE.

Turn a deaf ear to naysayers who tell you, "It can't be done." You've got inside intelligence! Jesus has told you that, with God, the impossible is possible! He'll equip you to do whatever you set your mind to. That's a great mindset! So, get busy today, and do the impossible!

I can do anything through You, Lord. Watch me go!

Evening

YES, I CAN!

How often do you tell yourself, "I can't"? Whether it's losing a few pounds, tackling that big home improvement do-it-yourselfer, or trying something new and scary, learn to say, "Yes, I can!" God knows that you can. Now, all you have to do is convince yourself. God will help you. Just start!

Dear God, when I tell myself that I can't,
remind me that I can. You said so, and I believe it!

MEMORY VERSE OF THE DAY

"Surely there is a reward for the righteous;
surely He is God who judges in the earth."

PSALM 58:11 NKJV

Morning

I'M SAVED TO DO GOOD WORKS.

You don't earn salvation by doing good works. Likewise, you are saved to do good works. Your "acts of righteousness" (godly living) should come as naturally to you as breathing. If your heart is linked to Christ, you should long to please Him in all you do. Is your heart linked to His today?

Jesus, my heart is linked with Yours today.
I hope to please You with everything I do.

Evening

GOD SMILES AT ME!

The reward for righteous living is a sense of satisfaction. When you please God with your actions, you're satisfied from the inside out, content that you're putting a smile on His face and bringing Him pleasure. When you make good choices, God smiles down on you. What a joyous way to live!

How wonderful, Father, that what I do can put a smile on Your face.
Smile down on me! Smile down on me tonight!

MEMORY VERSE OF THE DAY

"Therefore be merciful, just as your Father also is merciful."
LUKE 6:36 NKJV

Morning

HE TEACHES ME ABOUT MERCY.

Ponder this: God teaches us to be merciful by example. He picks us up and dusts us off after every tumble. No pointing fingers. No "Shame on you!" He simply brushes us off, gives us a holy hug, and leaves us feeling convinced that we're still loved, no matter what.

O, God, thank You for being such a gentle and loving teacher.
Thank You for showing me mercy.

Evening

I WILL BE MERCIFUL.

When you've received God's mercy time and again, it gets easier to extend it to others. Sure, you're still learning, but sooner or later, mercy will be a part of your character, something you won't even need to think about. Do you need to be merciful toward someone tonight? Ask God about it.

Lord, have I been too hard on someone?
Have I been too sparse with my forgiving? Who needs my mercy tonight?

MEMORY VERSE OF THE DAY

Beloved, I pray that you may prosper in all things
and be in health, just as your soul prospers.

3 JOHN 1:2 NKJV

Morning

I WILL PROSPER.

What does it mean to prosper? Acquiring lots of money? Simply having your needs met? If you look up the word "prosper," you will see that the definition includes the word "success." When you're successful, you're making progress, moving forward. Ask God to help you move toward success today. Trust that He will.

Lord, help me to move forward successfully. Help me to prosper.

Evening

SUCCESS IS MINE!

Prosperity has more to do with your spiritual condition than anything you could acquire with money. There's really only one way to prosper and find success—stick close to God, read and memorize His Word, and live by His precepts. Are you doing all these things? If so, then success will be yours!

Father, I am longing for a season of prosperity.
Will You help me to get there, please?

MEMORY VERSE OF THE DAY

Therefore, there is now no condemnation
for those who are in Christ Jesus.

ROMANS 8:1 NIV

Morning

I AM SECURE IN JESUS.

Your security is rooted in Christ's unconditional love for you. It is not based upon your performance but upon who He is. There is nothing that can separate you from His love including poor choices or disobedience. Nothing can pluck you from His hand. Jesus is yours, and you are His.

Dear Lord, my security comes in knowing You.
Thank You for Your enduring love!

Evening

NEVER CONDEMNED.

By accepting Jesus' gift of eternal life, you will never be condemned. He has prepared a home in heaven for you and has given you the indwelling Holy Spirit as a deposit guaranteeing that promise. That is the hope and assurance you can stake your life on. Rest secure tonight that He is with you.

O, Jesus! You are so wonderful. I am ever grateful
for Your gift of heaven and eternal life.

MEMORY VERSE OF THE DAY

"This is my command—be strong and courageous! Do not be afraid or discouraged. For the LORD your God is with you wherever you go."

JOSHUA 1:9 NLT

Morning —

I CAN HELP CHANGE THE WORLD.

In the Bible, women from all professions and backgrounds were changed by grace, and then, with the Holy Spirit's help, transformed the people around them. God wants to use you, too, in the same way. Does that thought scare you? Whatever He calls you to do, don't be afraid— He will equip you for the task.

Lord, help me be strong and courageous as I follow wherever You lead.

Evening —

GOD IS CALLING ME.

Women in every era have changed the world because they remained faithful to God and followed His leadership. Perhaps you've felt called to minister, and you wonder whether you've heard God right. Keep your eyes open; through circumstances, scripture, and mature Christian mentors, He will make clear the path He wants you to take.

God, I want You to use me to help change the world. Show me, please. What are You calling me to do?

MEMORY VERSE OF THE DAY

*I will always love you; that's why I've been
so patient and kind. You are precious to me.*

JEREMIAH 31:3–4 CEV

Morning

I AM PRECIOUS TO HIM.

Speak today's memory verse out loud while imagining to say it to your children.
No matter how naughty your children are sometimes, you continue to love them
because they are precious to you. That is exactly the way that God feels about
you. Even when you sin, You are His beloved, precious child.

*Lord, I sometimes wonder how You can love the sinful me,
but Your love is always there, and I revel in it!*

Evening

TRUE LOVE.

God's love for you is true. It's of the everlasting kind. And no matter what you do,
God will never stop loving you or love you less. Strong and powerful, His love is
unconditional. And you are His prized possession. Can you feel His love tonight?
Sit quietly, and soak it in.

*Heavenly Father, who am I that You, the Creator of the Universe, should love me?
But You do! Thank You for making me Your beloved child.*

MEMORY VERSE OF THE DAY

They were just trying to intimidate us, imagining that they
could discourage us and stop the work. So I continued
the work with even greater determination.

NEHEMIAH 6:9 NLT

Morning ———————————————

I WON'T BE DISCOURAGED.

Sometimes people will stand between you and your efforts to get the job done. The same thing happened to Nehemiah when he was building a wall around Jerusalem. But he prayed to God to strengthen his hands and turned all the discouraging chatter into his determination. You can do it, too!

Strengthen my hands, Lord.
Turn my discouragement into determination.

Evening ———————————————

I WILL BE DETERMINED.

What are your greatest goals? Are you determined to accomplish them? Determination takes hard work. The road to your goals will, likely, be filled with potholes. But God will be there to help you. So, pray, and ask Him to keep your determination going. . .and going. . .no matter what.

Father, when others say that I can't,
help me to be even more determined to try.

MEMORY VERSE OF THE DAY

The Lord doesn't need swords or spears to save his people.
The Lord always wins his battles, and he will help us defeat you.

1 Samuel 17:47 CEV

Morning

HE IS UNBEATABLE.

God, your amazing God, cannot be defeated. It's a spiritual law—the absolute truth! He is Master and Lord over everything and everyone. So the next time you face conflict, remember that God is unbeatable. And He's here to help you overcome any foes you face. Keep that in mind today!

Dear God, whenever I face an enemy,
I will look to You for help.

Evening

HE IS VICTORIOUS!

Your Almighty Father doesn't fight His, or Your, battles with weapons. He doesn't need them. All Your Father has to do is speak, and it will be so. God's way of fighting and winning is always perfect. He will help you to defeat your enemies—in His own way and His own time. Trust Him.

Lord, You are mighty and powerful in battle,
and always victorious. I trust You to help me.

MEMORY VERSE OF THE DAY

*"Most assuredly, I say to you, he who believes in Me,
the works that I do he will do also; and greater works
than these he will do, because I go to My Father."*

JOHN 14:12 NKJV

Morning

GREATER WORKS?

Today's verse is a tough one to accept. You might say, "What? I'm going to do greater works than Jesus?" Seems almost blasphemous, doesn't it? Still, the Lord might just use you to affect your world in a major way. It could happen. Brace yourself, because this is one promise that could leave you radically changed.

*Jesus, I believe everything You say. I will never be greater than You,
but I believe that You can use me to do great, even unimaginable, things.*

Evening

BELIEVE THE IMPOSSIBLE!

What if you had the faith to believe that nothing was impossible? Would you approach the situations around you differently? Tonight, ask God for the "extreme" faith required to believe today's memory verse. Ask Him to fill you with such great "belief in the impossible" that everything you encounter seems possible.

*God, my faith is strong, but I need it to be steel strong!
Give me extreme faith to believe the impossible.*

MEMORY VERSE OF THE DAY

*It is for freedom that Christ has set us free. Stand firm, then,
and do not let yourselves be burdened again by a yoke of slavery.*

GALATIANS 5:1 NIV

Morning

FREEDOM!

How do you earn freedom? You don't! Christ earned it for you on the cross.
All you have to do is accept Jesus as Savior of your life. Liberty begins in that
moment and lasts forever. You are no longer burdened by sin. Praise Jesus!
Celebrate your freedom today!

*Too often, Jesus, I take for granted my freedom from sin—
earned by You on the cross. Today and every day, I am grateful.*

Evening

MY CHAINS ARE BROKEN.

Today's verse says you can stand in complete freedom. Being "yoked" to sin (or
addiction) is akin to being in prison. You're locked away in your cell, unable to
break free. Then, suddenly, the chains are broken. Jesus breaks through the
prison walls and ushers you outside into ultimate freedom. Isn't it wonderful?

O, Jesus, thank You for freeing me from the chains of sin!

MEMORY VERSE OF THE DAY

*But now, this is what the LORD says—he who created you,
Jacob, he who formed you, Israel: "Do not fear, for I have
redeemed you; I have summoned you by name; you are mine."*

ISAIAH 43:1 NIV

Morning

HE KNOWS MY NAME.

Did you know that God knows your name? He created you. He knows you. He put together your personality and topped off His masterpiece by giving you all sorts of likes and dislikes, dreams and desires, passions and preferences. Celebrate, today, because you are His unique design, His child, His beloved one.

*What a miracle, God, that among all the world's people,
You know me, inside and out. You call me by name!*

Evening

I BRING HIM JOY!

Always remember that you belong to God. He takes great joy in you. You are His treasure. He sent Jesus to die on the cross to give you an abundant life. He wants to spend eternity with you! He calls you by name, and your name is music to your Father's ears.

Lord, I thank You for knowing my name and loving me unconditionally.

MEMORY VERSE OF THE DAY

*"But store up for yourselves treasures in heaven, where neither moth
nor rust destroys, and where thieves do not break in or steal;
for where your treasure is, there your heart will be also."*

MATTHEW 6:20–21 NASB

HIS PRIORITIES, NOT MINE.

Each day, you make choices about the priorities in your life. The world sends messages about how you should spend your time; however, if you listen to the still, small voice of God, you will learn how to "store up treasures in heaven." Quiet yourself and listen to His priorities today.

Eternal God, remind me of the importance of spending time with You.

Evening

STORING MY TREASURES.

Nurturing relationships and sharing Christ with others, as well as reading God's Word and getting to know Him through prayer, are examples of storing up treasures in heaven. Using your gifts for His glory is also important. The dividends of such investments are priceless. Meditate tonight on the gifts you have stored up in your heavenly home.

*Father, help me to store up treasures in heaven with the choices I make today.
Give me opportunities to show Your love.*

MEMORY VERSE OF THE DAY

So we say with confidence, "The Lord is my helper;
I will not be afraid. What can mere martals do to me?"

HEBREWS 13:6 NIV

Morning

DO YOU NEED A HELPER?

What are you facing today? Do you need a helper? God is the very best. Just knowing He's there will ease your mind and invigorate you for the tasks you face. And, if you remember today's and other encouraging Bible verses, they will boost your confidence and spur you on.

Lord, I'm so glad You stand nearby, whispering words of encouragement.

Evening

THE BEST HELPER EVER!

When you're up against a tough situation, God is standing right there, speaking positive words over you, telling you you've got what it takes to be the best you can possibly be. And while He won't take the reins—He wants you to learn from the experience —He will advise you as you go.

You're the best helper possible, God.
Thank You for taking my fears and replacing them with godly confidence.

MEMORY VERSE OF THE DAY

In your strength I can crush an army;
with my God I can scale any wall.

PSALM 18:29 NLT

Morning

THE FORCE IS WITH ME.

God gives you power to crush any obstacle you face. Think of it like scaling a high wall, one that you thought you would never get over. When you need a boost, an unseen force—God—fortifies your body, mind, and soul. By claiming today's promise, you can meet any challenge you face.

I need a boost today, Lord.
Give me Your strength to get over the hurdles.

Evening

I'VE GOT MUSCLE POWER!

Maybe you've never thought of yourself as having muscle power, but you do! In difficult, or dangerous, situations, God gives you the strength to overcome even the greatest force. Think of people who have escaped from disasters by praying and trusting the Lord for help. You have that kind of power, too!

I claim Your power, Lord. Help me overcome!

MEMORY VERSE OF THE DAY

*Whatever you ask for in prayer, believe (trust and be confident)
that it is granted to you, and you will [get it].*

MARK 11:24 AMPC

Morning

BELIEVE AND RECEIVE.

God doesn't want you to just ask Him for things. He wants you to trust Him to provide, to have confidence that He will deliver. So the formula is, believe and receive! The best thing is, the more you receive, the more you will believe. What an awesome paradox!

I believe, Jesus. I believe!

Evening

GOD, DO WE AGREE?

God will always provide for your needs. If you ask for something that isn't good for you, He will put what He knows is best before what you want. So, always ask God to help you to pray in accordance with His will. If you and He are in agreement, you *will* get what you've asked for.

*Father God, is what I am asking for in line with Your will?
If not, then take that desire from me and replace it with something even better.*

MEMORY VERSE OF THE DAY

The LORD gives you rest from your sorrow,
and from your fear.

ISAIAH 14:3 NKJV

Morning

GOD'S PEACE.

Don't go through today feeling poorly. When sorrow, pain, and fear develop within you, the Lord will give you His peace. All you need to do is reach out to Him. He'll give you the touch you need. By focusing your mind, heart, and soul on Him, your problems will recede.

Lord, today I need the peace found only in You.

Evening

HE GIVES ME REST.

How was your day? Sometimes, life events cause so much emotional pain that it's impossible to have a good day. But God can help with that. Focus on today's memory verse. Repeat it multiple times until it plays over and over in your mind. Then, trust God to give you rest.

Heavenly Father, You are my Comforter.
I trust and believe that You will give me rest from my troubles tonight.

MEMORY VERSE OF THE DAY

*God never changes his mind about the people
he calls and the things he gives them.*

ROMANS 11:29 NCV

Morning —

FOREVER GIFTS.

Think about this: You've just received a great present, but after awhile, it becomes ordinary, and you use it less and less. The gift giver says, "Hey, if you're not going to use that, I want it back." Aren't you glad God isn't like that? When He gives you gifts (spiritual gifts/talents/abilities) they are forever.

*Almighty God, thank You for all that You have given me,
and thank You that Your gifts are forever.*

Evening —

I WILL USE MY GIFTS TO SERVE HIM.

When you actively use God's gifts, He's so pleased! But if your gifts lie dormant for a season, God won't take them back. The gifts He has placed inside of you are a blessing to you and to others. And the Lord knew exactly who He could trust with them—you!

*God, renew my enthusiasm for the gifts You've given me.
I want to use them to serve You well.*

MEMORY VERSE OF THE DAY

A wise man is strong, yes, a man of knowledge increases strength.
PROVERBS 24:5 NKJV

Morning

JUST LIKE POPEYE!

Do you remember Popeye the Sailor Man? One can of spinach, and. . .bam! His muscles plumped up, his strength increased, and he acquired the courage to face his enemies. God's children get their strength not from spinach, but from the wisdom found in His Word. So, swallow a little wisdom today.

Dear Lord, I want to grow in godly wisdom,
so speak to me through Your Word, the Bible.

Evening

WISDOM MAKES ME STRONG.

Read from the book of Proverbs tonight. If you spend time growing in godly wisdom, your strength—knowledge of God's will—increases. You will garner strength to whip your enemies, though not necessarily physical ones. Strong in spirit, you can defeat the enemy of your soul when he tries to attack.

God, just keep pouring Your wisdom into my brain!
I want to be strong and ready when the enemy shows up.

MEMORY VERSE OF THE DAY

In Him also we have obtained an inheritance,
being predestined according to the purpose of Him
who works all things according to the counsel of His will.

EPHESIANS 1:11 NKJV

Morning

GOD CHOSE ME.

Have you inherited something special? Maybe you received your grandfather's Bible or your dad's class ring. Such gifts are treasures. But, as wonderful as they seem, you have an inheritance that is far greater—God's gift of eternal life. Think about it: He chose *you* even before the foundation of the world. Wow!

Thank You, Father, for Your gift of eternal life.
Thank You for wanting it for me.

Evening

I'LL TAKE MY INHERITANCE, PLEASE.

Jesus left you the best gift when He died on the cross for your sins. If you haven't already, you can take hold of your inheritance right now—tonight—and it will change your life, not just now, but for all eternity. Eternal life—Jesus wants you to have it!

Jesus, I'm sorry for the sin in my life. I'm amazed that You want to be my
Savior forever. I'm ready to accept my inheritance, right now!

MEMORY VERSE OF THE DAY

"Consider how the wild flowers grow. They do not labor or spin. Yet I tell you, not even Solomon in all his splendor was dressed like one of these. If that is how God clothes the grass of the field, which is here today, and tomorrow is thrown into the fire, how much more will he clothe you—you of little faith!"

LUKE 12:27–28 NIV

Morning

HE LOVES ME MORE!

If God makes flowers, each type unique and beautiful, and if He sends rain and sun to meet their needs, won't He care for you, too? He made you. What the Father makes, He loves. And that which He loves, He cares for. You are dearer to God than any of His other creations.

O, Lord, how wonderful it is that I am more special to You than any of Your other creations!

Evening

GOD TAKES CARE OF ME.

Look up at God's creation. He made the night sky with such intricate detail. Rest in Him now. Trust Him. Just as He cares for His moon and stars, His flowers and birds, God is in the business of taking care of His children. Let Him take care of you.

Father God, I will rest well in You tonight, being certain that You will take care of me.

MEMORY VERSE OF THE DAY

*But do not forget this one thing, dear friends: With the Lord a day
is like a thousand years, and a thousand years are like a day.*

2 PETER 3:8 NIV

Morning —————————

THROUGH GOD'S EYES.

Today's memory verse is all about time and patience. Ponder it: *With the Lord
a day is like a thousand years, and a thousand years are like a day.* If you often
become discouraged with waiting, 2 Peter 3:8 gives you a fresh perspective. It
helps you to see your life through God's eyes.

*Heavenly Father, patience is hard for me sometimes, so make it easier
by helping me to understand "heaven's time."*

Evening —————————

A BIBLICAL PERSPECTIVE.

Are you feeling worried, burdened, or overwhelmed tonight? Take a step back
and look at the big picture. Ask God to give you some of His perspective.
Adopting a biblical viewpoint on your circumstances can mean the difference
between peace and anxiety, and between sorrow and joy.

*While I wait, I will remember, God,
that everything You do is according to Your perfect timing.*

MEMORY VERSE OF THE DAY

Every man's work shall be made manifest: for the day shall declare it, because it shall be revealed by fire; and the fire shall try every man's work of what sort it is.

1 CORINTHIANS 3:13 KJV

Morning

GET INVOLVED!

Do you genuinely wish to help bring glory to God? If you get involved in an act of service, you will be blessed beyond measure. We are all called to be useful for Christ. When we do so willingly and with a servant's heart, the joy that fills us will be indescribable and lasting.

Jesus, open my eyes today to those with a servant's heart.
I want to learn from them how to be useful for You.

Evening

I WILL SERVE WITH A PURE HEART.

When you serve, do it with a pure heart dedicated to God's work, and not to receive praise and recognition. God blesses those who serve out of love, wanting nothing in return. God knows your heart. He will recognize your motives and reward you accordingly. Tonight, plan ways to serve Him.

Lord, I want to serve You with a pure heart. Let all I do bring glory to You.

MEMORY VERSE OF THE DAY

This is the day which the LORD hath made;
we will rejoice and be glad in it.

PSALM 118:24 KJV

Morning

GOOD MORNING!

It's a new day! A new opportunity to build on yesterday's endeavors or to make a totally brand-new start. So get your morning off on the right foot. Rejoice! Be glad! Go forth with a smile on your face, a praise song on your lips, and joy in your heart!

Lord, thank You for this marvelous day!

Evening

EVERY DAY IS A GIFT.

Today's memory verse is one that you should wake up reciting tomorrow and every morning. Whether you wake up wishing that you could sleep until noon, or whether you wake up ready to tackle the day, it is important that you acknowledge God's gift of a new day. You are alive! Be happy!

Dear God, I don't ever want to take for granted the gift of another day. Thank You!

MEMORY VERSE OF THE DAY

Forget what happened long ago! Don't think about the past.

ISAIAH 43:18 CEV

Morning

LOOK TO THE FUTURE.

When you keep looking behind you, at mistakes and hurts that occurred in your past, you're bound to trip up in the present. God wants you to keep your eyes open, looking to the future. He is going to do a new thing. You might even get a few hints from Him today.

God, help me to let go of the past and focus on the future.

Evening

I'M STUCK!

Dwelling on the past is like being stuck in quicksand. You just keep sinking deeper and deeper, praying for someone to come along and pull you out. You have that someone! God is right there waiting to grab your hand and renew your faith in the future. Reach out. He's waiting to save you.

Father, sometimes I find myself stuck in the past.
Take my hand, please, and set me on the path to my future.

MEMORY VERSE OF THE DAY

He arose and rebuked the wind and said to the sea, Hush now!
Be still (muzzled)! And. . .there was [immediately]
a great calm (a perfect peacefulness).

MARK 4:39 AMPC

Morning

JESUS, I NEED YOU!

Do you think Jesus is sleeping on the job? He isn't! Jesus is always ready to calm any storm that comes into your life. Have you cried out to Him lately? If not, do so! Get down on your knees and shout for help. Before long, the storm will fade away, and you will be calm.

The storm is too much for me, Lord! HELP!

Evening

"HUSH NOW! BE STILL!"

Your thoughts may be the storm that's rocking your peace. Tonight, imagine Jesus in a boat with you. Your thoughts rise, like angry waves, but Jesus stands up and rebukes them. "Hush now! Be still!" You feel His presence. You know that you're safe. Soon you'll be drifting off to perfect, peaceful sleep.

Dear Jesus, tonight, when I lie down,
please calm my thoughts and bless my sleep with peace.

MEMORY VERSE OF THE DAY

*For he has rescued us from the dominion of darkness
and brought us into the kingdom of the Son he loves,
in whom we have redemption, the forgiveness of sins.*

COLOSSIANS 1:13–14 NIV

Morning ————————————————————

OUT OF THE DARKNESS.

God will rescue you from your darkest days. Imagine wandering in pitch darkness knowing your enemy lurks there. Then, a shaft of light breaks through, sending the enemy running. You are lifted—physically, spiritually, and emotionally—to a place surrounded by warm "Sonlight" on every side. That's what it's like when God rescues you.

*Dear God, whenever darkness covers me and I feel afraid,
I know that You will rescue me.*

Evening ————————————————————

RESCUED BY SALVATION.

Oh, to be rescued by the Author of Light! To be transferred to a new "kingdom," one where God's Son illuminates your path. Through His gift of salvation, God promises to split through the bleak, dark shadows and lift you to a new place, one where His goodness and radiant light are ever-present.

*I praise You, Father, for lifting me from the darkness
into the radiant light that is Your Son, Jesus.*

MEMORY VERSE OF THE DAY

*"They will fight against you but will not overcome you,
for I am with you and will rescue you," declares the LORD.*

JEREMIAH 1:19 NIV

Morning

GOD IS BIGGER.

Remember when you were a kid, how someone's size could intimidate you? A bully seemed meaner because he was bigger than the other guys. And if he had an older/bigger brother, look out! Here's good news: No one can out-size God! He's bigger than any foe you could possibly face, so you have nothing to fear.

*Father, Your greatness, Your bigness,
protects me from evil. My trust is in You.*

Evening

STEP ASIDE.

God wants to replace your anxieties with His peace—the kind of peace that says, "Hey, calm down! I've got this. Let me handle it for you." Sure, you'll still have troubles. Bullies will raise their ugly fists. But if you'll step aside and let God handle them, your troubles will resolve themselves in a hurry.

*I forget, sometimes, to step aside and let You handle my troubles, Father.
I will try to remember—will You help me?*

MEMORY VERSE OF THE DAY

*Let the wicked forsake his way, and the unrighteous man his thoughts;
let him return to the LORD, and He will have mercy on him;
and to our God, for He will abundantly pardon.*

ISAIAH 55:7 NKJV

Morning

GUILTY AS CHARGED.

Imagine that you are accused of a crime you're guilty of. But the judge declares you innocent, ready to pardon you, no questions asked. You can go free. You are blessed to receive a second chance. This is what God does for you every time you ask for His forgiveness. Think about it!

*O, God, I am so blessed by Your forgiveness of my sins.
Thank You for second. . .and third. . .and fourth chances! I love You!*

Evening

PARDONED!

When God sent His Son, Jesus, to the cross to die for your sins, He pardoned you from your sins. Suddenly the things you'd done wrong—the lies, the pain you'd caused others—were washed away. Not only that, but your pardon included an all-expenses paid trip into eternity! How wonderful is that?

*I treasure Your gift of salvation, Jesus.
My words cannot express how wonderful You are.*

MEMORY VERSE OF THE DAY

And the words of the Lord are flawless,
like silver purified in a crucible, like gold refined seven times.

PSALM 12:6 NIV

Morning

GOD'S WORD IS FLAWLESS.

"Perfection." It's a word we use lightly, but what does it really mean? For something to be "absolutely perfect" means that it is flawless. God is flawless, and so is His Word. Every verse you have memorized, every word of it, is flawless today and forever. Nothing on earth compares.

Lord, Your Word is perfect in every way.
As I read and learn scripture, teach me so that I may serve You well.

Evening

NOTHING BUT THE TRUTH.

The Bible is 100% true. You can trust every word. Spend time tonight thinking about the promises you have memorized. All of them are God's gifts to you—so claim them as your own. As you read your Bible, stop and think of it as God's love letter to you. Treasure His words in your heart.

Dear Father God, thank You for the Bible—
my one and only guidebook for life!

MEMORY VERSE OF THE DAY

Take the sword of the Spirit, which is the word of God.

EPHESIANS 6:17 NLT

Morning

HIS INSTRUCTIONS ARE CLEAR.

The Bible is filled with valuable information for your mission on earth. God's Word can set your mind at peace and hold you steady through life's storms. The truth found within its pages is your assurance that no matter what you face in this battle of life, God will bring you safely home.

I'm grateful, God, that Your instructions for my earthly mission are clear, trustworthy, and faultless. Thank You!

Evening

GOD'S WORD IS MY PERSONAL TRUTH.

Take a new approach to God's Word. Let it breathe new revelation—new life— into your heart. Expect knowledge and understanding of His Word to become personal, written just for you. Anchor your soul by believing what you read, and know that the promises from God assure that the victory belongs to you.

God, I know the Bible is true and full of wisdom for my life. Help me to grow and understand what I read and apply it to my life.

MEMORY VERSE OF THE DAY

*You are a letter from Christ. . . . This "letter" is written not with pen
and ink, but with the Spirit of the living God. It is carved
not on tablets of stone, but on human hearts.*

2 Corinthians 3:3 nlt

Morning

I AM A LETTER FROM JESUS!

You might be the only Bible a person will ever read. You are a letter from Christ!
When you share your faith, be more than a hasty e-mail: Be a precious letter from
Jesus and take time to let others know how loved and treasured they are by the
Lord.

*Father, help me to make the people in my life feel loved and cherished.
Help me to remember that I am a letter from You as I interact with others.*

Evening

A TICKET TO HEAVEN.

Jesus sent His disciples on a mission to spread the Good News. You are His
disciple, too. Watch for opportunities every day to act in a Christ-like way and to
share with others why Jesus is so important in your life. Who knows? You might
just be someone's ticket to heaven.

*Jesus, I don't want to be shy about sharing my faith.
Teach me how to share You with others, at the right time and in the right way.*

MEMORY VERSE OF THE DAY

*Daniel answered and said: "Blessed be the name of God
forever and ever, for wisdom and might are His."*

DANIEL 2:20 NKJV

Morning

I WON'T TAKE HIM FOR GRANTED.

Read about Daniel in the Bible, and you will discover his many trials. He came close to death more than once, but God always saved Him. And Daniel didn't take that for granted! He reacted with worship and thankfulness. Think about this today: How do you react when God steps in and helps you?

*Make me thankful, Lord, for all the ways in which You bless and care for me.
I don't want my life to become laden with ungratefulness.*

Evening

BLESSED BE THE NAME OF GOD!

Though God is great, He doesn't appreciate being taken for granted any more than you would. God doesn't just help in life-and-death situations, like Daniel's. He takes care of smaller troubles, too. Tonight, spend time thinking about all the little things God does for you every day—and give thanks!

*O, God, thank You for my heart that beats,
my lungs that breathe, my eyes that see. . .and so many other things!*

MEMORY VERSE OF THE DAY

*You are my hiding place; you will protect me
from trouble and surround me with songs of deliverance.*

PSALM 32:7 NIV

Morning

HE IS MY HIDING PLACE.

Look around you and find a place to rest today. When you have found it, then look to Jesus. He is your hiding place, a haven, a quietness in the midst of a busy day. Give the Lord your worries, your troubles, and your questions. Give Him your praise and thanksgiving, too!

Jesus, be my refuge today, my hiding place, my place of rest.

Evening

SING TO ME, JESUS!

When your day has been especially long, ask your Savior to sing over you. He promises to sing songs of deliverance to you. Like a mother sings lullabies and rocks her baby to sleep, so your Redeemer longs to hide you from the pressures of this great big world and give you peaceful rest.

*After a long day, Lord, I feel so weary.
Bring me rest, I pray. Sing songs of deliverance over me.*

MEMORY VERSE OF THE DAY

We are more than conquerors through Him who loved us.

ROMANS 8:37 NKJV

 Morning

GOD'S LOVE CONQUERS.

No matter what happens today, you will *not* be defeated. Nothing can keep you from God's love. It will always be with you, pulling you up off the ground and into victory—today and every day! Look for His love today. It might come straight to your heart or through someone else.

I am amazed at Your unfailing love, Lord.
With You on my side, I will not be defeated!

Evening

"MORE THAN."

When you memorized today's verse, did you notice those words "more than"? They are powerful words! You don't just conquer your enemies (your problems), but you *more than* conquer them. You send them to Your heavenly Father, who squashes them like a bug. God's love strikes your troubles dead!

Father, Your love more than conquers my problems.
You strike them dead so that I can move on. Thank You!

MEMORY VERSE OF THE DAY

"May you be richly rewarded by the LORD. . .
under whose wings you have come to take refuge."
RUTH 2:12 NIV

Morning ───────────────────────────

RUN TO HIM.

When you feel bruised, beaten, and battered by the world, run to the Lord. He will give you shelter under His wings, mend your wounds, and give you rest. As you abide in Him, you will find peace, comfort, and rewards uncountable. If things get tough today, run to Him.

Lord, I run to You today.
I thank You for making me whole again!

Evening ───────────────────────────

MY FAITH IS REWARDED.

When you were a child, maybe an unfamiliar situation or a loud noise left you running to the shelter of your mother's arms. Just because you are an adult now doesn't mean that you don't need someone to run to. God is the One! And He rewards you for your faith in Him.

Almighty God, my faith is in You,
and I find peace and contentment in the shelter of Your arms.

MEMORY VERSE OF THE DAY

God doesn't lose his temper.
He's powerful, but it's a patient power.

NAHUM 1:3 MSG

Morning

HE IS PATIENT WITH ME.

God gets angry sometimes, but He can control His temper. That's why humans are still here. How's your temper? Are you as just in your anger with others as God is with us? Perhaps it's time to stop fuming and start forgiving. Give that some thought this morning.

Dear God, please help me to keep my anger in check today.
I want to be a peacemaker, not a fighter.

Evening

GIVE IT TO GOD.

Anger is another of those "give it to God" things. As soon as you feel agitated, long before you reach the boiling point, give your anger to God. Ask Him to help you react to the situation in a godly way that brings Him glory. The way you react will be, perhaps, a teachable moment for others.

Father, the next time I feel like losing my temper,
show me how to react in a gentle and loving way.

MEMORY VERSE OF THE DAY

Be strong, alert, and courageous. . .and work!
For I am with you, says the Lord of hosts.

HAGGAI 2:4 AMPC

Morning —

THE GOOD OLD DAYS.

When times get tough, people start to look back to the good old days. But God doesn't want you to get stuck reminiscing or wondering what could've, should've, or would've been. He wants your mind and eyes looking ahead, scouting out new opportunities. What new opportunities lie ahead for you today?

Help me to look forward, Lord,
seeking the new opportunities You've set before me.

Evening —

CONSIDER THE GOOD THINGS.

Tonight, make a list of all the good things happening in the world, and then thank God for them. Concentrate on good news: stories about people who are strong, alert, and courageous. And what about workers in your community? Thank God for them, too. Ask God to open your eyes to all the goodness in His world.

Heavenly Father, make me blind to the bad things tonight.
Open my heart and mind only to what is right and good.

MEMORY VERSE OF THE DAY

She is clothed with strength and dignity,
and she laughs without fear of the future.

PROVERBS 31:25 NLT

Morning

I CAN LAUGH AT THE FUTURE.

God wants you to be assured of His care, to the point of your being able to laugh at the future. He's told you that nothing can harm you. So what is there to fear? Gird yourself with His strength. Take joy in the day. Have a good guffaw with God!

My heart is filled with joy and laughter, for You are my God!

Evening

CLOTHED IN STRENGTH AND DIGNITY.

What a gift to face a catastrophe with power and poise. This gift from God comes as a result of faith and also the assurance of His love. Whether it's an illness, death of a loved one, or whatever, when you trust in God, a beautiful coat of strength and dignity is yours.

Almighty God, help me to face whatever trials come my way.
Clothe me in strength and dignity.

MEMORY VERSE OF THE DAY

"I've said it, and I'll most certainly do it.
I've planned it, so it's as good as done."

ISAIAH 46:11 MSG

Morning —————————————————————

HE DOES WHAT HE'S PROMISED.

How are you at keeping promises? Sometimes people don't mean their promises. Or they mean them but somehow don't come through. God isn't like that. What He says, He'll do—you can be certain of it. So dig into His promises. Go forth this morning with confidence that they're as good as done!

I trust You, Lord, like no other,
knowing You'll make good on Your promises to me!

Evening —————————————————————

YOU CAN COUNT ON ME.

Imagine today's memory verse as your promise to someone. Will you absolutely make good on that promise? Maybe you've promised someone something, but you didn't follow through. Apologize to that person. Then, if it's possible, make good on your promise. It will put a smile on your Father's face—and also the face of the person you wronged.

Father, forgive me for the promises I haven't kept, both to You and to others.
Help me to make good on those promises wherever I can.

MEMORY VERSE OF THE DAY

Our mouths were filled with laughter,
our tongues with songs of joy.
PSALM 126:2 NIV

Morning

GOD LOVES GIGGLES.

From a small giggle that you keep to yourself to a great big belly laugh, laughter is a wonderful stress reliever and a blessing from God. How many times have you been in an awkward situation or in a stressful position and laughter erupted to break the tension? Thank God for laughter today.

Heavenly Father, I love knowing that You like laughter.
Thank You for every giggle and guffaw.

Evening

GO ON, HAVE A GOOD LAUGH!

God made humans to experience great joy. Our design didn't include carrying stress, worry, and heaviness every day. When was the last time you really had a good laugh? Have you laughed so hard that tears rolled down your cheeks? Go ahead! Ask God to give you a really good laugh tonight.

Lord, help me rediscover laughter.
Help me to take every opportunity You bring to see the joy in life every day.

MEMORY VERSE OF THE DAY

*Moses' arms soon became so tired he could no longer hold them up.
So Aaron and Hur found a stone for him to sit on. Then they stood on each
side of Moses, holding up his hands. So his hands held steady until sunset.*

EXODUS 17:12 NLT

Morning

A LITTLE HELP FROM MY FRIENDS.

Moses, following God's instructions, stood on a hill holding up the staff of God.
As long as he held it, arms high, the Israelites were winning in a battle with their
enemy. When Moses arms became tired, his friends Aaron and Hur rushed in to
help. How might you help a friend today?

*Dear God, today's memory verse is a good reminder of
the importance of friendship. Help me to be a good friend today.*

Evening

WONDERFUL FRIENDSHIP!

Friendship is a wonderful thing. Think about your best friends tonight. Were
there times when you've "held up their arms"? Have they held up your arms in
your times of greatest need? Write a letter or note to thank your friends for their
friendship. Then thank God for best friends!

*Thank You, heavenly Father, for my best friends.
You did a great job choosing them for me!*

MEMORY VERSE OF THE DAY

"Worship and serve him with your whole heart and a willing mind.
For the LORD sees every heart and knows every plan
and thought. If you seek him, you will find him."

I CHRONICLES 28:9 NLT

Morning

I WILL WORSHIP AND SERVE HIM.

What is your idea of success? God's view of success might be vastly different than yours. You will find true success in earnestly seeking after Him and following His commands. He asks that you give yourself to Him in worship. So seek God today—worship and serve Him willingly.

Dear Lord, teach me to seek after You willingly,
with sincere motives.

Evening

REAL SUCCESS.

God focuses on your journey. You may not live in a big, beautiful house, or drive a new car, but those things are not important to God. Instead, worshipping and serving Him with your whole heart, being genuine and sincere, and willingly seeking Him—that's *real* success in God's eyes. How successful are you?

Please help me, God, to focus on pleasing You,
rather than seeking success by worldly standards.

MEMORY VERSE OF THE DAY

The highway of the upright is to depart from evil;
he who keeps his way preserves his soul.

PROVERBS 16:17 NKJV

Morning

FOLLOW THE RIGHT ROAD.

Life is a journey. There is a right road, and also detours—sin that distracts you from the path God has laid for you. Trust God to guide you today! In prayer, reflection, and self-examination, He will show you any wrong turns you took and set you back on the right path.

O, God, give me grace to repent when I have strayed.
Turn me back on the right path.

Evening

HE WILL SHOW ME THE WAY.

Tonight, sit in silence and listen for God's voice. Ask Him what He wants for you. What is the destination for your heart? Are you staying on the right road? Do you need to set some boundaries for yourself so you can better hear His voice? He is ready to show you the way.

Father, help me to be still, to sit in silence and listen for Your voice.
Show me the boundaries I need for my life.

MEMORY VERSE OF THE DAY

Adam and his wife hid themselves from the presence of the LORD God amongst the trees of the garden. And the LORD God called unto Adam, and said unto him, Where art thou?

GENESIS 3:8–9 KJV

Morning ————————————————————————

WHERE ARE YOU?

Throughout the Bible, God asks us questions inviting us to dialogue with Him. The very first question God asked called Adam and Eve to self-awareness. "Where are you?" Of course, God knew where they were. He wanted to make *them* aware. Think about it: Where are you in your relationship with God?

Father God, I long for a deeper relationship with You. Here I am!

Evening ————————————————————————

HE MEETS ME WHEREVER I AM.

God still whispers, *Where are you?* He wants to spend time with you, but you get buried in the routines of everyday life—and another appointment with Him gets broken. The more appointments you break, the easier it becomes to forget. Take a moment to answer God's question. He will meet you wherever you are.

Dear heavenly Father, teach me the discipline of spending time with You.
Let me listen and answer when You call.

MEMORY VERSE OF THE DAY

Jesus used many. . .stories and illustrations to teach
the people as much as they could understand.

MARK 4:33 NLT

Morning

BIBLE STORIES.

The Bible is filled with true stories about people facing all kinds of situations. As you read about kings, queens, battles, and banquets, meditate on the stories just as you meditate on your daily memory verses. Remember—God often uses His stories in the Bible to teach you about your own life.

Lord, I'm guilty of skimming over some of the true stories in Your Word.
Help me to focus on them and the messages You have for me within them.

Evening

I WILL MEDITATE ON HIS WORDS.

Jesus often taught using parables—little stories with a lesson. But the lesson wasn't always clear. Jesus wanted people to use their brains and think about His words. And that is what He wants you to do as you memorize scripture. Are you thinking about His words and applying them to your life?

Jesus, if memorizing scripture ever becomes mundane,
remind me of the importance of meditating on Your words!

MEMORY VERSE OF THE DAY

"Give your entire attention to what God is doing right now, and don't get worked up about what may or may not happen tomorrow. God will help you deal with whatever hard things come up when the time comes."

MATTHEW 6:34 MSG

Morning —————————————————————

WHAT ARE YOU WORRYING ABOUT?

Is worry zapping you of your energy? More than eighty-five percent of what you worry about will never happen. What a waste of power! So instead of wringing your hands, retool and refuel by fixing your eyes on the present and what God is doing right now. Your energy will increase hands down!

Energize me, Lord, and keep me focused on what You are doing right now!

Evening —————————————————————

GOD IS IN CHARGE OF MY LIFE.

If worry is keeping you awake, remember that God is in charge of your life and everything that affects it. Whatever it is that is keeping you awake, God is working it all out, right now. Trust in His timing instead of your own. Give Him your worries, and go to sleep!

Lord, help me to trust that You have everything under control.
Grant me rest tonight as I leave my worries in Your capable hands.

MEMORY VERSE OF THE DAY

"Don't be afraid. Just stand still and watch the Lord rescue you today. The Egyptians you see today will never be seen again."

Exodus 14:13 NLT

Morning

I WILL KEEP MY COOL!

The problems or people that plague you today will one day disappear from view. So keep your cool. Don't be afraid or give in to the fight-or-flight reflex. Rest assured that God is handling the situation for you. All you have to do is keep still and watch Him work today.

Lord, I know You are working in this situation. Thanks for taking it off my hands!

Evening

GOD TO THE RESCUE!

Poof! That problem you face right now is already gone, in God's eyes. He has it under control and already solved. You might not see His solution yet, but it's coming. You can trust that! "God to the rescue!" That should be your motto. Remember it. Say it to yourself often.

Father God, I know that You already have this problem solved. So, give me peace while I wait for Your solution.

DAY 328

MEMORY VERSE OF THE DAY

"Stop doubting and believe."

JOHN 20:27 NIV

Morning ————————————————————

RECHARGE MY BELIEF!

Today's memory verse is short, but, oh, so important! God knows that doubting decreases your faith. Believing revs it up. Where are you on the belief meter today? Need to be recharged? Tap into the conduit of faith by committing this simple verse to memory. Then stop doubting and believe!

Almighty God, help me to stop doubting and to trust in You, even more!

Evening ————————————————————

SONGS OF WORSHIP AND PRAISE.

Along with memorizing today's scripture verse, choose a hymn or worship song that really speaks to your heart. Memorize the words, and sing them until the song plays over and over in your head. It will not only reenergize your belief, but also be a comfort in times of trial.

Lord, thank You for the many hymns and worship songs available to me.
I will sing them to worship and praise You.

MEMORY VERSE OF THE DAY

"Because of your faith, it will happen."
MATTHEW 9:29 NLT

Morning

FAITH BRINGS DESIRES INTO REALITY.

Today's memory verse is another short but powerful one, another promise from God. Memorize it and ponder it. When your desires are in line with God's will, then your faith is what brings those desires into reality. Think about that today. Because of your faith—it *will* happen! Believe it!

Father God, set my desires in line with Your plans for me.
Then give me faith to believe it will happen.

Evening

FAITH VS. FEELINGS.

Meditate on this tonight: What has the upper hand in your mind, heart, soul, and spirit—faith or feelings? If you have faith that God is able to do anything and everything, He will do it! Faith brings victory while feelings bring defeat. Make a plan to be victorious with faith.

Lord, I believe You are able to do anything! I have faith!

DAY 330

MEMORY VERSE OF THE DAY

Jesus Christ is the same yesterday, today, and forever.
HEBREWS 13:8 NLT

Morning

YESTERDAY, TODAY, AND FOREVER.

Change is everywhere, and although change can be good, not knowing what the future holds can be unsettling. Where you live can change. Jobs can change. Relationships can change. But there is one relationship that will never change—your relationship with Jesus. He is the same yesterday, today, and forever!

Dear Jesus, I take comfort in knowing that while other things change in my life, You will remain the same.

Evening

JESUS, MY STEADFAST SAVIOR.

Changes will come, but Jesus will be there through each one, remaining the same always and forever. Tonight, think about all the changes that He has already brought you through. With His help, you got through them all! Keep allowing His steadfastness to give you peace in this ever-changing world.

Thank You, Jesus, for bringing me through all the changes in my life. I love and trust in You!

MEMORY VERSE OF THE DAY

*We do not want you to be uninformed about those who sleep in death,
so that you do not grieve like the rest of mankind, who have no hope.*

1 Thessalonians 4:13 NIV

Morning

GRIEVE WITH HOPE.

Sometimes we get the impression that grieving or crying implies that we don't trust God, that we don't believe He has everything under control. However, in today's memory verse, Paul teaches on the subject of death and is clear: grieve, but not without hope. Can you give a grieving friend hope today?

Thank You, Jesus, for understanding the pain of grief and for loving us through it.

Evening

GO AHEAD, CRY!

Perhaps you are the one in need of hope tonight. Is your heart heavy over a recent loss? Go ahead. Cry your heart out. Jesus feels your pain, and your tears are precious to Him. But when you grieve, be sure to grieve with hope in the coming of our Lord.

My Savior, when I grieve, helps me to do so with hope.

MEMORY VERSE OF THE DAY

*Let no one look down on your youthfulness, but rather in speech,
conduct, love, faith and purity, show yourself an
example of those who believe.*

I TIMOTHY 4:12 NASB

Morning

I WILL BLESS THEM WITH WORDS.

God hears the conversations of His children. As you spend time with others and speak with one another, your Father wants your words to bless the lives of those who participate. He wants you to build others up with the words you use. So, get out there this morning and build someone up!

Jesus, please touch my lips and allow nothing dishonorable to pass through them.

Evening

MY WORDS WILL GLORIFY HIM.

Ponder this tonight: Unbelievers will watch and listen, always looking to find Christ in the lives of those who profess His name. So always be careful to share God's faithfulness, goodness, and love when you speak, because your conversations have an impact in the lives of everyone around you.

*Lord, guide me and give me grace and discernment in my conversations
so that they will always give glory to Your name.*

MEMORY VERSE OF THE DAY

When he saw the crowds, he had compassion on them because they were confused and helpless, like sheep without a shepherd.

MATTHEW 9:36 NLT

Morning

MEET THE GOOD SHEPHERD.

Reach out and introduce someone to the Good Shepherd today. Live your life before others with authenticity and humility. Allow others to see God's peace in times of trials, the Father's comfort in times of grief, the Savior's hope in times of uncertainty. Be real so you can point others to Christ.

Jesus, I will do my best to live in a way that others see You through me.

Evening

A HEART TURNED TOWARD JESUS.

We need the Lord's eyes to see people's hearts. Then compassion will compel us to reach out. People need to know that they are loved unconditionally, that God has a purpose for their lives, and that God can guide them along life's journey. Whom do you know who needs their heart turned toward Jesus?

Dear Lord, open my eyes to see the lost sheep around me.
Help me to lead them to You.

MEMORY VERSE OF THE DAY

God is not a God of confusion but a God of peace.

1 CORINTHIANS 14:33 NCV

 Morning

WORLDLY CLUTTER.

How are you feeling this morning? Is worldly chaos getting the best of you? Are you confused about what to do? When chaos and confusion rule your life, serenity goes out the door and stress moves in. Do yourself a favor. Rid your life of worldly clutter and watch the peace rain in!

Dear Jesus, please help me to put aside the worldly clutter and set my thoughts on You.

Evening

GET RID OF THAT MESS!

God doesn't bring confusion into your life—Satan does that. He loves to surround you with litter. Look around. Do you see clutter? Maybe your physical surroundings are uncluttered, but your heart is a mess! Ask God to give you the wisdom to get rid of it. Strive for an uncluttered life.

I want a simpler life, God. Give me the wisdom to declutter my life!

MEMORY VERSE OF THE DAY

"Do not worry about your life, what you will eat or drink;
or about your body, what you will wear."

MATTHEW 6:25 NIV

Morning

WHAT SHOULD I. . .?

What should I wear to the wedding? What should I make for dinner when company comes? Do you stress out with questions like those? Today's memory verse reminds you not to worry about such things. Keep it simple. Keep your eyes on God, and He will take care of the rest.

God, help me to keep my eyes on You.

Evening

GOD IS IN THE DETAILS.

When you begin asking yourself "What should I" and What if" questions, then it's time to seek God's wisdom. He has planned every detail of your life—yes, even what you should eat, drink, and wear! So seek His wisdom. Allow Him to guide you in everything you do.

Heavenly Father, too often I forget that You care about even the smallest
details of my life. Forgive me! Guide me with the details.

MEMORY VERSE OF THE DAY

Before daybreak the next morning,
Jesus got up and went out to an isolated place to pray.

MARK 1:35 NLT

Morning

MY FIRST PRIORITY TODAY.

Jesus knew what to do to refuel. In the still hours of the morning, He went off by himself to a secluded place to connect with His Father. Follow His example, and you'll find your energy and devotion increase tenfold! Make meeting with your heavenly Father your first priority today and every day.

Father God, I reach out for You at the start of this new day.

Evening

ALONE WITH GOD.

Tonight, after your family has gone to bed, find a place where you can come to the Lord alone while everyone else is asleep. Soak up the stillness and pray. You might find that in the night when you are alone with God, your bond with Him grows even stronger.

Here I am, God. Meet me in the stillness. Speak Your sweet words to my heart.

MEMORY VERSE OF THE DAY

By day the LORD directs his love, at night his song is with me—
a prayer to the God of my life.

PSALM 42:8 NIV

Morning

HE CONDUCTS MY LIFE.

Your life is like a symphony. There are some highs and some lows, and God is there directing it all. During the daytime—when most of the major decisions of life are made—He's there, leading you, guiding you. Keep your eyes on His baton, and let His love direct you today.

I don't want to carry the baton, Lord.
Willingly remove it from my hands. Direct me today.

Evening

HE CALMS ME WITH HIS SONG.

Allow the Lord—your Conductor—to lead you through the highs and lows, the crescendo moments and the pianissimo ones, as well. Then when night shadows fall, listen closely for the song He's playing over you. His song is like a lullaby that calms you from the stress of the day and guides you into sleep.

Oh, Father! I can almost hear the music now.
Sing Your song over me tonight.

MEMORY VERSE OF THE DAY

God, God, save me! I'm in over my head.

PSALM 69:1 MSG

Morning ───────────────────

CRY OUT TO GOD.

Are you in over your head? Then cry out to God. You need Him this day, this hour, this moment! You need the One who made you and knit you together in your mother's womb. You need Him to save you—from yourself. Cry out to Him now. He hears you.

Dear God, come and save me.
My burden overwhelms me, and I'm in over my head.

Evening ───────────────────

SAVE ME!

"God, God, save me! I'm in over my head," the psalmist wrote. And in the twenty-first century, you can relate to his plea! Ask God to lift from you the burdens you've created for yourself so you might focus again on what's important—Him! Ask God to help you rest in His goodness.

Father, I realize I have lost You in the shuffle.
Help me to find You, I pray.

MEMORY VERSE OF THE DAY

Jesus called the children to him and said, "Let the little children come to me, and do not hinder them, for the kingdom of God belongs to such as these."

LUKE 18:16 NIV

Morning

CHILDLIKE FAITH.

To enter the kingdom of God, one must receive Him like a little child. What is childlike faith? It's an innocent, fearless faith. It's a kind of pure, unsoiled trust that leaves no room for distrust or sarcasm. Childlike faith doesn't have to be accompanied by a ton of Bible knowledge. A simple "I believe Jesus is the Christ, the Son of God" is all it requires.

Jesus, I believe that You are God's Son, and I am Your child. Take care of me today. Teach me, guide me, and love me!

Evening

I WILL RUN TO JESUS!

As you begin to grow in faith, you learn to put your complete trust in God and His Word. You are Jesus' child. You can always depend on Him. His arms will always be there to hold and to keep you safe. Run to Him tonight with childlike faith, without any fear or doubt.

Dear Jesus, I'm so glad that I'm Your child. Help me to always have that childlike faith that is pleasing to You.

MEMORY VERSE OF THE DAY

"In the desert you saw how the LORD your God carried you, like one carries a child. And he has brought you safely all the way to this place."

DEUTERONOMY 1:31 NCV

Morning

SAFELY HOME.

Are you wondering where God is in the midst of your trials? He's right there with you! Reflect on the way He delivered you from trouble in the past. Know that He loves you and that He will carry you out of trouble again and again and again, until you're safely home.

God, my arms are reaching out to You.
Pick me up and carry me safely home.

Evening

HE WON'T LET ME FALL.

When you are in trouble, God stands ready to lift you into His arms, and He knows precisely when to do it. Sometimes He allows you to fight the battle for a while, to build your strength and faith. But rest assured, your Father won't let you fall. He'll always carry you to safety.

Father God, when trouble comes my way,
I trust You to lift me up and keep me safe.

MEMORY VERSE OF THE DAY

"Observe what the LORD your God requires:
Walk in obedience to him. . .so that you may prosper in all you do."

I KINGS 2:3 NIV

Morning

DO WHAT GOD WANTS.

You don't have to be half-Vulcan like Star Trek's Mr. Spock to know how to "live long and prosper." Just check out God's Word. It has the formula, and it's a simple one to remember: Do what God wants you to do—you'll not only expand God's Kingdom but flourish in the process!

Show me what You want me to do, Lord.
I'm ready to prosper!

Evening

FOLLOW THE LEADER.

As a child, did you play Follow the Leader? When you did what the leader said, you were okay, but if you didn't follow the leader's ways, you were out—lost! Walking in God's ways is similar to the game. The big difference is that it's real and you might risk being lost forever.

Lead me, Father, and I will follow in Your footsteps.

MEMORY VERSE OF THE DAY

Though a host encamp against me, my heart will not fear;
though war arise against me, in spite of this I shall be confident.

PSALM 27:3 NASB

Morning

FOCUS ON JESUS.

When an army of evil comes marching against you, surrounding you on every side, don't be afraid. Fear gives the enemy an edge, because your focus will be on them instead of God. Keep your Rescuer, Jesus, in focus. He'll lift you out of the fray and deal with the enemy, too!

Jesus, my Rescuer, lift me up and away from evil.
Protect me from my enemies.

Evening

HE IS MY CONFIDENCE.

Maybe you don't feel safe in today's world. God doesn't want you to be afraid. Instead, He wants you to be confident that He's with you. Not only is God with you, but He also has charge of the situation. In wars, terrorist attacks, even attacks on your heart, God is your confidence. You will prevail.

God, You are my confidence. When evil comes my way,
I will remain sure that You are in control.

DAY 343

MEMORY VERSE OF THE DAY

*Honor the LORD from your wealth and from the first
of all your produce; so your barns will be filled with plenty
and your vats will overflow with new wine.*

PROVERBS 3:9–10 NASB

Morning

I WILL PUT GOD FIRST.

God is not a God of leftovers. He wants you to put Him first. One way to honor God is to give Him your "firstfruits," the best you have to offer. Remember: everything you have comes from God. The Bible calls you to give back to the Lord one-tenth of all you earn.

Lord, remind me not to separate my finances from my faith.

Evening

I WILL HONOR THE LORD.

Read these words: *Honor the Lord. . .from the first of all.* Giving to God has great reward. You may not have barns you need God to fill, but you will reap the benefit in other ways. When you honor God by giving to Him, you can trust that He will provide for your needs.

*Heavenly Father, all that I have comes from Your hand.
I will honor You with my firstfruits.*

MEMORY VERSE OF THE DAY

His wife's name was Abigail.
And the woman was intelligent and beautiful in appearance.

1 Samuel 25:3 nasb

Morning ─────────────────────────

WISE ABIGAIL.

God blessed Abigail with wisdom. In the Bible, her brains are mentioned before her beauty. And how well she used her brain! She stood before a furious king and his army, calming him with just her words. Think about Abigail today. Read about her in the Bible. What can you learn from her?

Dear God, thank You for using the people in the Bible to teach me
about my own life. Thank You for the gift of Your Word.

Evening ─────────────────────────

ASK GOD FOR WISDOM.

Just as He granted Abigail the wisdom to soothe a king, the Lord will grant you the wisdom and intelligence to handle whatever today's world throws at you. Wisdom is different from being "book smart." It comes from God speaking to your heart. Listen to Him tonight. What is He telling you to do?

Lord, grant me the wisdom and grace to deal with
my family, my home, and my work.

MEMORY VERSE OF THE DAY

For thus said the Lord GOD, the Holy One of Israel, "In returning and rest you shall be saved; in quietness and in trust shall be your strength."

ISAIAH 30:15 ESV

Morning

I DEPEND ON GOD.

What is your definition of "strength"? God's Word gives His view of strength—rest, quietness, and trust. These words all reflect a state of dependence. Strength comes when you acknowledge your weakness and your need for God, ending your self-reliance, and trusting Him for your needs. Strength, at its core, is depending on God.

Father, remind me today that You are not asking me to be strong, but to depend on You.

Evening

HE IS MY STRENGTH.

When your sin overwhelms you, you repent and turn to God for forgiveness. When you are weary of trying to earn His favor, you stop and remember that you only have to receive His grace. In solitude, you hear Him speak, you learn to pray, and in trusting Him, you become strong.

*In my weakness Lord, You are my strength.
Help me to return, rest, listen, and trust.*

MEMORY VERSE OF THE DAY

*I am certain that God, who began the good work within you,
will continue his work until it is finally finished.*

PHILIPPIANS 1:6 NLT

 Morning ───────────────────────────

I AM A PRICELESS WORK OF ART!

Although you may not be where you want to be think today about how far you've come. Consider that you are God's work in progress. He is continually working within you, carefully shaping you into the person He wants you to be. You are His work of art, priceless and one-of-a-kind!

Thank You, Creator, for shaping me into Your unique work of art. I love You!

Evening ───────────────────────────

NEVER TOO OLD TO CHANGE.

God will continue working on you until the moment when you become perfect with Him in heaven. You will never be too old or too wise for Him to stop tweaking His vision of you. Be aware of His changes within you—some big, some little, but all of them good!

*God, keep working on me and making me as close
to perfect as I can be on this side of heaven.*

MEMORY VERSE OF THE DAY

For my thoughts are not your thoughts,
neither are your ways my ways, saith the LORD.

ISAIAH 55:8 KJV

Morning

GOD KNOWS BEST.

You may not understand everything that happens in your life, but God does. After all, He's the Supreme Being, the only God, and He knows so much more than any human ever will. It's unfathomable. Just rely on His good judgment. He has what's best for you in mind. Believe it!

Lord, I don't understand it all.
But thanks to You, I don't have to!

Evening

WHEN BAD THINGS HAPPEN. . .

When bad things happen, you ask, "Why?" What God allows might be a mystery to you, but you can be certain that He understands how it fits into His plan. Sometimes when you ask why, God has no answer. He requires that you just trust Him and not lose faith. Can you do that?

O, dear Father, when I don't understand,
give me strength to trust You and not lose faith.

MEMORY VERSE OF THE DAY

Be my strong refuge, to which I may resort continually; You have given the commandment to save me, for You are my rock and my fortress.

PSALM 71:3 NKJV

Morning

HE IS MY CONSTANT REFUGE.

God isn't available to save you just once in a while. He's your constant refuge. Minute by minute, hour by hour, day by day, anytime you need Him, God is there. So, run to Him. Hide in Him. Return to Him, again and again, to build up your strength.

Here I am, Lord. Thank You for always being here for me.

Evening

A MIGHTY FORTRESS.

Imagine a fortress, a heavily protected and impenetrable structure. Nothing, not even a nuclear attack can destroy it. No one can overtake it. But someday, it will become old and crumble away, just like everything on earth. God is not that kind of fortress. His protection is forever!

You can count on that.

Almighty God, You are my fortress, my protector.
Nothing can stop You from shielding me from evil.

DAY 349

MEMORY VERSE OF THE DAY

"Who knows? Maybe you were made queen for just such a time as this."
ESTHER 4:14 MSG

Morning

WHY AM I HERE?

To live in God's will is no easy task. At some point, you wonder, *Why am I here? What does God want from me?* Like Queen Esther in today's memory verse, you need to examine your life and consider. . .maybe God brought you to this very place for such a time as this.

Father, please show me the purpose for my day today.

Evening

OPPORTUNITY ALERT!

God wants you to be sensitive to opportunities that help make a difference for His kingdom. Every day, keep your eyes open for these opportunities. Big or small, the choices you make to help others just might be God's purpose for you here on earth. Meditate on that tonight.

*Lord, open my eyes to the opportunities that You put before me
to make a difference in other peoples' lives.*

MEMORY VERSE OF THE DAY

"Love one another, even as I have loved you."

JOHN 13:34 NASB

Morning

A PERFECT KIND OF LOVE.

You tell Jesus you love Him, and His response is, "I love you more." You cannot comprehend that kind of love, yet you are the recipient of it! He loves you not because of anything you've done, but because of His goodness. Isn't it reassuring to know that God loves you with a perfect, limitless love?

Jesus, thank You for Your love for me.
I hope You know that I love You, too!

Evening

NO ONE IS UNLOVABLE.

Jesus is love itself. He commands you to love others in the same way that He loves you. We all have unlovable people in our lives. But Jesus doesn't see anyone as unlovable. Look at that difficult-to-love person through new eyes tonight, and love him or her as Jesus has loved you.

Forgive me, Jesus, for not loving others in that same way.
Give me the ability to love others as You have instructed.

MEMORY VERSE OF THE DAY

"What no eye has seen, what no ear has heard, and what no mind has conceived"—the things God has prepared for those who love him.

1 Corinthians 2:9 NIV

Morning

THAT'S NOT WHAT I EXPECTED.

Maybe you doubt the direction you felt God urging you to pursue. Don't quit! Don't give up! Press on with your dream. Failure isn't failure until you quit. When it looks like it's over, stand strong. With God's assistance, there is another way, a higher plan, or a better time to achieve your dream. Trust Him!

God, thank You for putting dreams in my heart. I refuse to quit.

Evening

FOCUS ON THE DREAM MAKER.

Think about this tonight: God knows the dreams He has placed inside of you. He created you and knows what you can do—even better than you know yourself. Maintain your focus—not on the dream but on the Dream Maker—and together you will achieve your dream.

Father, I'm looking to You to show me how to reach my dreams.

MEMORY VERSE OF THE DAY

*Make it your ambition. . .to live quietly and peacefully,
to mind your own affairs, and to work with your hands.*

1 Thessalonians 4:11 AMPC

Morning

TAP INTO CHRIST'S PEACE.

Do you want a peaceful, quiet day? You can have one by tapping into Christ's peace and minding your own business. Keep your mouth shut when you know you should, and your mind on your work; and, before you know it, others will want what you have, and God's kingdom will grow!

*Jesus, thank You for Your peace.
May it spread today like Son—shine!*

Evening

AMBITION TAKES HARD WORK.

Today's memory verse says to make it your "ambition" to live quietly and peacefully. Ambition requires determination and hard work. Think about today. Were your conversations quiet and peaceful? Did you raise your voice or speak harsh words? Did you mind your own business? Ask God to help you to aim for a quiet, peaceful life.

*God, I long to live a peaceful,
quiet life that reflects Christ's character. Please help me.*

MEMORY VERSE OF THE DAY

I said to myself, "Relax and rest. GOD has showered you with blessings.
Soul, you've been rescued from death; Eye, you've been rescued
from tears; and you, Foot, were kept from stumbling."

PSALM 116:7 MSG

Morning

GOD CHAT.

Talking to yourself lately? That's okay—as long as you're feeding yourself positive, uplifting thoughts. When you assure yourself of God's blessings and heed His instructions to allow your mind, body, and soul to relax, it's like a healing balm. Keep up the God chat all day long. It does you good!

Thank You, Lord, for Your healing words.

Evening

SHOWERS OF BLESSINGS.

Get into the habit of reciting today's verse every night before you pray. Reflect on all the blessings of the day, and thank God for them. Think especially about all the unseen blessings that you've missed. Praise God for taking such good care of you! Then relax and get some rest.

Father, thank You for so many blessings today.
Open my eyes to the ones I've missed.

MEMORY VERSE OF THE DAY

You shall be a blessing. Fear not, but let your hands be strong.

ZECHARIAH 8:13 AMPC

Morning

I'M A BLESSING!

God thinks you are a blessing. That's a great compliment from the Almighty! Just be brave and keep up the good work. You are going to change this world for the better, and God won't let anything stand in your way. Now, get out there today, and be someone's blessing!

Thanks for the encouragement, Lord. With You, I cannot fail!

Evening

I "SHALL."

Don't you love encouraging Bible verses like today's? God promises that you "shall" be a blessing. That means He will use you to do His good work. All you have to do is be brave, be open to hard work, and trust God with the rest. Have you been a blessing today?

O, Lord, I'm brave, ready to work,
and my trust is in You. Use me, please, to bless others.

MEMORY VERSE OF THE DAY

She thought, "If I just touch his clothes, I will be healed."
MARK 5:28 NIV

Morning ————————————————————————

THE POWER OF A TOUCH.

Remember that you should never underestimate the power of a touch. In today's memory verse, the true power of a simple touch is beautifully portrayed. Think about this: a touch communicates not only affection, but also affirmation and sympathy. Today, you might encourage people—or comfort them—with a godly touch.

Lord, I turn to You when I need comfort.
Let me also offer those around me the comfort of a loving touch.

Evening ————————————————————————

A LITTLE HUG OR KISS.

Maybe you've rushed from one appointment to another, skimping on affection with your family. You waved good-bye to your children without a hug. Your spouse headed off to work with the slight brush of a kiss. Tonight, hold those you love. Hug them. Let them see a bit of Jesus' love in you.

Dear Jesus, a gentle hug or a little kiss means so much to my loved ones.
Forgive me for times when I've withheld a loving touch.

MEMORY VERSE OF THE DAY

To fear the LORD is to hate evil;
I hate pride and arrogance, evil behavior and perverse speech.
PROVERBS 8:13 NIV

Morning ————————————————————————

FEAR GOD?

Why does the Bible say to "fear" God? In reality, to fear God is not the same as fearing a creepy-crawly spider inching up the living room wall. Instead, to fear God means we have a deep respect and reverence for Him. He is the Almighty, the Creator of the Universe, and He deserves respect.

I kneel before Your throne with the deepest respect for You,
my Lord and my King.

Evening ————————————————————————

STAND IN AWE.

Take time tonight to stand in awe of the One who deserves your utmost respect and love. Your life should reflect deep reverence for your heavenly Father—and love for your Creator, bursting forth in joy! Honor Him every day with humility, godly behavior, and clean speech.

Lord, help me to make my daily actions and speech reflect my respect for You.

MEMORY VERSE OF THE DAY

It is vain for you to rise up early, to sit up late,
to eat the bread of sorrows: for so he giveth his beloved sleep.

PSALM 127:2 KJV

Morning

SLEEP— GOD'S GIFT.

How did you sleep last night? Sleep is a gift from God. He bestows it on you for health. Think about this: Ignoring sleep is faithlessness. Long nights of work, play, or worry, show that you don't trust God to provide for your needs. He says, "Sleep, and I will take care of the rest."

Thank You, Father, for giving me Your gift of sleep.

Evening

BEDTIME!

Not only will God take care of your concerns while you sleep, but He also promises new mercies each morning (Lamentations 3:23). You don't have to go to bed when the sun goes down. You can sit up late doing anything you want. But don't! Accept God's gift of sleep, and go to bed!

Father, let me rest in You tonight, knowing that You will provide for my needs.

MEMORY VERSE OF THE DAY

*"She has done what she could. . . . What this woman has done
will also be spoken of in memory of her."*

MARK 14:8–9 NASB

Morning

I WILL DO WHAT I CAN.

God does not require that you be perfect—you can't be! All He asks is that you do what you can. But before you jump in to be a doer or a fixer, ask God to guide you. Ask Him to lead you to do what you can in alignment with His will. Then, act!

*Father God, sometimes I forget to seek Your guidance before I act.
Help me to remember, please.*

Evening ——————————————————

LOVE IS MY MOTIVE.

When Christians do what they can with love as their motive, their actions are recognized by Jesus and stick in the memories of others. Be bold in your worship of God and service to others. Never mind what people say. You, having done what you could, will be commended by your Father, Himself.

*Lord, I have done all that I can, and now, I leave the rest up to You.
Speak to my heart if I can do more. I long to serve You.*

MEMORY VERSE OF THE DAY

Though I have fallen, I will rise.
*Though I sit in darkness, the L*ORD *will be my light.*

MICAH 7:8 NIV

Morning

LIGHTER DAYS.

Do not give up during the dark days of your life. Keep trusting that the Lord will raise you up after you fall. He will turn your trials into blessings. Better and lighter days lie ahead, so continue seeking His presence today, knowing that He will make things right.

Lead me out of the wilderness and into Your light, O Lord.

Evening

I WILL RISE.

"I will rise." Those are powerful words from today's verse. They remind us that Jesus rose from the dead. They also hint at other Bible stories in which Jesus' miracles caused people to rise from their deathbeds. So continue to have faith. Believe that you will rise above any trouble you face.

I will rise above my problems, heavenly Father.
I will rise because You help me.

MEMORY VERSE OF THE DAY

*O Lord, You are our Father; we are the clay, and You our Potter,
and we all are the work of Your hand.*

ISAIAH 64:8 AMPC

Morning ────────────────────────────

GOD IS THE POTTER.

Hold tight to this thought today: God is constantly working on your spiritual shape, transforming you hour after hour, day after day, year after year. You are a work in progress. Make yourself pliable in His hands and before you know it, you'll be a beautiful work of art!

*Keep working on me, Lord.
Make me utterly beautiful in Your sight!*

Evening ────────────────────────────

PUTTY IN HIS HANDS.

You've probably heard someone say, "I am putty in his hands." That's not always a good thing. Sure, parents, teachers, and mentors help to shape you, but when someone tries to mold you into what they want you to be, it's not right. Trust God. Be putty in *His* hands, but no one else's.

*Shape me, mold me as You see fit, Lord.
I am putty in Your hands!*

MEMORY VERSE OF THE DAY

"Beware! Guard against every kind of greed.
Life is not measured by how much you own."

LUKE 12:15 NLT

Morning

JESUS IS MY EVERYTHING!

The Lord never meant for you to be satisfied with temporary treasures. Earthly possessions leave you empty because hearts are fickle. Once we gain possession of one thing, our hearts yearn for something else. Remember this today: Lasting treasure can only be found in Jesus. Jesus is enough. Jesus is everything!

Dear Jesus, You are my "enough."
You are my everything!

Evening

TRUE WEALTH.

When Jesus becomes your treasure chest, hope is in Him rather than net worth. Joy comes by walking with Him, not by chasing a fleeting fancy. He showers love upon you as you grab hold of a life that cannot be bought, but that can only be given through Him. That's true wealth!

Jesus, may I not wish for more material treasures,
but seek eternal wealth from You.

MEMORY VERSE OF THE DAY

There is no fear in love. But perfect love drives out fear, because fear has to do with punishment. The one who fears is not made perfect in love.

1 JOHN 4:18 NIV

Morning

PERFECT LOVE.

Perfect love is like light. God's love for you is perfect. It is complete. The sacrifice of His Son to reconcile you to Himself is the ultimate act of His love. Jesus came to you in your sinfulness, loving you first so that you could love Him. Feel His love! Let it shine!

Jesus, my Savior, fill me with Your love today.
Let it shine through me so others see.

Evening

HOW DEEP IS GOD'S LOVE?

Do you know how deeply God loves you? He says that nothing can separate you from His love—not suffering, distress, persecution, famine, nakedness, danger, or war. Allow the light of God's love to shine into the dark corners of your mind tonight, chasing away any fear that dwells there.

Lord, help me to know more of Your deep and complete love for me.

MEMORY VERSE OF THE DAY

*"For truly, I say to you, until heaven and earth pass away,
not an iota, not a dot, will pass from the Law until all is accomplished."*
Matthew 5:18 esv

Morning

PERFECT POWER.

Today's memory verse reminds you of the perfect power of God's Word—the Bible. It is God's Law for living, and Jesus said that every word of it is true and alive until that day when God brings our world and His heaven to His ultimate forever.

*God, Your Word is the ultimate power and strength.
It is my direct line to Your wisdom. Thank You!*

Evening

BOUND UP IN LOVE.

Someday our earth and heaven will no longer exist. God will create a new heaven and a new earth (Revelation 21:1). There, everyone who has accepted Jesus as their Savior will dwell with Him. Jesus said, "Blessed are those who obey the words of prophecy written in this book" (the Bible). Read tonight: Revelation 22:7–21.

Come, Lord Jesus! I am so grateful that we are forever bound up in Your love.

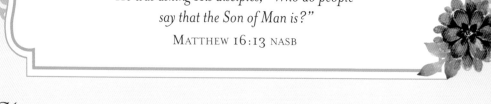

DAY 364

MEMORY VERSE OF THE DAY

*Now when Jesus came into the district of Caesarea Philippi,
He was asking His disciples, "Who do people
say that the Son of Man is?"*

MATTHEW 16:13 NASB

Morning ────────────────────────────

EVERYONE IS WATCHING!

Just as people watched Jesus in His lifetime, people are watching you. What are people saying about you? What do your actions tell them about you and your relationship with God? Jesus' words and teachings were powerful, but it was His actions that caused others to stop and take notice. What will people see in you today?

Lord, thank You for reminding me that I represent You in everything I do.

Evening ────────────────────────────

ACTIONS SPEAK LOUDER.

What matters most isn't really what you say, although words are important—it's what you do that speaks loudest in the lives of those around you. Who do others say you are? And does what you do each day point people to Christ? Your reputation precedes you. Take inventory of your influence tonight.

*God, help me to make godly choices
and good decisions to influence others to see You in my life.*

MEMORY VERSE OF THE DAY

You have heard me teach things that have been confirmed by many reliable witnesses. Now teach these truths to other trustworthy people who will be able to pass them on to others.

2 Timothy 2:2 NLT

Morning

I WILL TEACH HIS TRUTHS!

You've memorized 365 scripture verses! Each has taught you a biblical truth and brought you nearer to God. The truths you've stored in your heart are your arsenal for whatever trouble comes your way. But God isn't done with you yet! He wants you to share these truths with others.

Lord, I will be Your disciple.
Today, and every day, I will live as a reflection of You.

Evening

MY HEAVEN–BOUND GUIDEBOOK.

Tonight, meditate on what you have learned from these memory verses. Have they changed you? How have you seen God work in your life? Have you shared His Word with others? Plan to continue to read and learn from God's Word—the Bible—every day. Make it your heaven-bound guidebook.

O, Father God, thank You for teaching me. Now, lead me into a lifetime with You.
Help me to grow in faith and serve You every day.

10:41...Day 71

12:15...Day 361

12:27–28...Day 300

18:16...Day 339

18:27...Day 280

John

1:12...Day 109

3:3...Day 261

3:16...Day 237

3:17...Day 157

5:24...Day 180

7:38...Day 147

10:2–3...Day 90

10:10...Day 107

13:34...Day 350

14:12...Day 289

14:16–17...Day 38

14:27...Day 259

15:16...Day 11

16:24...Day 121

16:33...Day 104

17:16...Day 263

20:27...Day 328

21:21–22...Day 215

Acts

3:5...Day 253

3:19...Day 243

13:38...Day 174

13:51...Day 234

17:28...Day 17

Romans

3:23...Day 251

5:1...Day 101

4:20–21...Day 129

6:14...Day 248

8:1...Day 284

8:28...Day 65

8:31...Day 186

8:37...Day 314

8:38–39...Day 217

8:39...Day 21

11:29...Day 297

12:8...Day 176

Discover the Power of Prayer

Power Prayers Devotional
Scripture encourages us to "come boldly unto the throne of grace" (Hebrews 4:16)—and this *Power Prayers Devotional* will help with 180 inspiring prayer starters. These powerful meditations encourage women of all ages and backgrounds to approach God in intimate, joyful, confident prayer. Whenever you say, "Here I am, Lord," He is thrilled to listen to your deepest hopes and fears. Start on your journey of truer, deeper, more effective communion with the Lord whose love for you is everlasting.
DiCarta / 978-1-61626-608-0 / $14.99

Power Prayers to Start Your Day Devotional Journal
This delightful journal from Barbour Publishing fits perfectly into a woman's prayer life. Journalers will find themselves encouraged and inspired to record all of the ways they are blessed and loved by their heavenly Father. Fabulous as a gift—or for personal use—this journal will be cherished for years to come.
DiCarta / 978-1-63409-636-2 / $17.99

Power Prayers Coloring Book
Color your way to a more powerful prayer life with the brand-new *Power Prayers* coloring book. Dozens of unique images on quality stock will comfort and inspire through beautiful design and refreshing prayers. The backs of each generous 8x10 coloring page are left blank—perfect for coloring with crayons, colored pencils, and markers.
Paperback / 978-1-63409-968-4 / $9.99

Find These and More from Barbour Books
at Your Favorite Bookstore
www.barbourbooks.com

BARBOUR
PUBLISHING